PROSPERITY THINKING

Recession-Proof Thinking

Dr. Larry E. Gallamore
and Dr. Jan Burke Gallamore

BALBOA
PRESS
A DIVISION OF HAY HOUSE

Copyright © 2011 Dr. Larry E. Gallamore and Dr. Jan Burke Gallamore.

All rights reserved. No part of this book may be used or reproduced by any means, graphic, electronic, or mechanical, including photocopying, recording, taping or by any information storage retrieval system without the written permission of the publisher except in the case of brief quotations embodied in critical articles and reviews.

ISBN: 978-1-4525-3728-3 (sc)
ISBN: 978-1-4525-3730-6 (e)
ISBN: 978-1-4525-3729-0 (hc)
Library of Congress Control Number: 2011913652

Balboa Press books may be ordered through booksellers or by contacting:

Balboa Press
A Division of Hay House
1663 Liberty Drive
Bloomington, IN 47403
www.balboapress.com
1-(877) 407-4847

Because of the dynamic nature of the Internet, any web addresses or links contained in this book may have changed since publication and may no longer be valid. The views expressed in this work are solely those of the author and do not necessarily reflect the views of the publisher, and the publisher hereby disclaims any responsibility for them.

The author of this book does not dispense medical advice or prescribe the use of any technique as a form of treatment for physical, emotional, or medical problems without the advice of a physician, either directly or indirectly. The intent of the author is only to offer information of a general nature to help you in your quest for emotional and spiritual well-being. In the event you use any of the information in this book for yourself, which is your constitutional right, the author and the publisher assume no responsibility for your actions.

Any people depicted in stock imagery provided by Thinkstock are models, and such images are being used for illustrative purposes only.
Certain stock imagery © Thinkstock.

Printed in the United States of America

Balboa Press rev. date: 8/10/2011

CONTENTS

PART ONE

Introduction 3

Chapter 1   The Wildest Thing Any Human Being Has Ever Discovered 7
Chapter 2   Moving Toward a Higher Consciousness 14
Chapter 3   Change Your Outer World by Changing Your Inner Thoughts 18
Chapter 4   What Does it Mean to be Spiritual? 22
Chapter 5   The Steps to an Awakened Life 29
Chapter 6   Life Becomes Cold When There is No Magic in It 33
Chapter 7   Renew Your Life by Renewing Your Mind 39
Chapter 8   Change Your Thinking and Change Your Life 44
Chapter 9   The World of Reality 50

PART TWO

Chapter 10   Achieving Prosperity 57
Chapter 11   The Human Mind Has No Boundaries 63
Chapter 12   You Were Born to be Prosperous! 67
Chapter 13   Prosperous People Learn to Live by the Laws of Achievement 70
Chapter 14   Learn How to Communicate with Your Subconscious Mind 73
Chapter 15   You'll Want to Have More Than You Need So You Can Share with Others 78
Chapter 16   How to Attract Prosperity 83

Chapter 17	Once Prosperity is Yours, Look for New Opportunities for Additional Prosperity 88
Chapter 18	The More You Help Others to Be Prosperous, the More Prosperous You will Become 93
Chapter 19	Enjoy Your Prosperity with Careful, Pleasurable Spending..97
Chapter 20	Prosperous People Like Money, They Just Don't Fall in Love with It..99
Chapter 21	How Prosperity Thinking Works................................102

Endnotes...105

PART ONE

INTRODUCTION

The whole world is on the eve of a new consciousness and a renewed discovery of the resources within the Self. These resources have always been available to us and were known to humankind centuries ago, but somewhere along the way, they were laid aside and emphasis was placed on the physical part of humanity. Thus, we began to look to the material world to explain why we are the way we are, why things turn out the way they do, and we look to the material world for answers to life's problems. Many people have accepted the lie that we are limited in what we can accomplish; believing only people born to riches can accomplish much. Others must accept whatever life hands them. We look to physicians, professors, scientists, psychologists and a myriad of experts for the answers to life's problems. The purpose of this book is to reacquaint you with the resources you have within you, and get you to look within for the answers to life's problems instead of trying to find the answers outside your "self". The answers aren't out "there". They are inside you. These answers are at your disposal twenty-four hours a day, seven days a week, 365 days a year. They are with you in your waking and in your sleeping. They are just waiting for you to tap into them, to consult them, to ask your questions. You will, then, get the answers you need.

Our twenty-first century is positioned to produce the greatest progress mankind has ever known in mental and spiritual power. The most powerful forces of mankind will be manifested by those who follow universal laws and who recognize how life really works. Invisible forces will manifest themselves through human minds as we learn more and more about the power of thoughts and how our inner thoughts produce our outer circumstances.

As we were writing this book, we began to hear the dire predictions of economic recession and as we thought about it, it became clear to us that this book contains the answer to the question, "How can we deal effectively with the recession. How can families get through the recession and thrive in spite of it? It seems apparent that our leaders in government do not know what to do to get us out of the recession. We have to take responsibility for ourselves. We can't wait for them to come up with the answers. They are bound by the laws of politics. We aren't! The short answer to the question of how we get through the recession and thrive is to follow the laws of the universe, which will be introduced in Part One of this book and apply them to every area of your life which will be discussed in Part Two. You will read throughout this book that what a person thinks inside, will be manifested or brought to life in their outer circumstances. If you think failure, you will experience failure. If you think success, you will experience success. What you focus on will be fulfilled in your life. The good news is when fifty-one percent of the world starts to apply prosperity thinking, we will find the recession lifting. Better economic times will be on the horizon.

In Part One, you will be introduced to the idea of a life without limitations. This is the end result of Prosperity Thinking. If you change your practice of thinking to Prosperity Thinking, you will live a life without limitations. The only limitations you have are the limitations you place on yourself through your thoughts. Part One discusses the theory of Prosperity Thinking and goes into great detail of the importance of how and what you think and the effect it has on your life. We think constantly but most of the time we are unaware of all the thoughts that are going through our minds. This section is intended to wake you up. Be alert to what you are putting into your mind every minute of every day. What you think is significant and essential to how you live your life and what you are able to accomplish. Be careful what you think. What you think, matters. Chapter Three discusses this at length. If you want to change your outer circumstances, change your thoughts.

Part Two focuses on the idea and techniques of Prosperity Thinking. DISCLAIMER: THIS IS NOT A GET-RICH QUICK BOOK. So many infomercials about getting rich quickly and effortlessly have been on television that many people shy away from anything that speaks of prosperity, causing prosperity to be thought of as greed, but this is a misunderstanding of the concept of prosperity. Prosperity is much more than material wealth as Part Two illustrates. We can be prosperous in all areas of life: health, relationships with family, friends, and coworkers; job satisfaction, career fulfillment, life satisfaction, mental health, and so on. You will learn how the subconscious mind works and how it is essential in our living. You will also learn how the subconscious mind and conscious mind work together. You will learn how to attract prosperity and the benefits that your prosperity can bring to the lives of others.

In this book, you will learn how Prosperity Thinking can turn failure into success. You will learn how to substitute thoughts of peace, courage, power, inspiration and harmony and how to remove thoughts of failure, despair, and limitation from your subconscious mind before they manifest into your outer world.

As prosperity thoughts take root in your life, your brain cells will be physically changed and you will start to see life in a whole new light. You will attract to yourself new and successful associates, new circumstances, new conditions, and you will find real life in places you least expect. You will discover an inner power within, a power that will give you a great advantage over the struggles that are apparent in all of life.

You'll discover that your world without is a reflection of your world within. In your world within, you will find Infinite Wisdom, Infinite Power, and an infinite supply of all that is necessary for a prosperous life.

You'll discover it was through the subconscious mind that Shakespeare perceived great truths that were hidden from the conscious mind, sculptor Phidias learned to fashion marble and bronze, artist Raphael painted his masterpieces, and Beethoven composed great symphonies. These great people and countless others used their subconscious mind to connect to the Creative Intelligence of the Universal Mind.

We invite you to join us on this amazing adventure of prosperity-thinking. Change your thinking and you will change your life. Through reading this book and applying the principles, you can open the door to prosperity and enjoy good health, satisfying relationships with family, friends, and coworkers; experience career fulfillment and have true abundance in all areas of your life. Once you open the door to prosperous living, your life will open up in ways you never dreamed possible.

And now, turn the page and let the journey begin.

Dr. Larry E. Gallamore
Dr. Jan Burke Gallamore

CHAPTER 1

The Wildest Thing Any Human Being Has Ever Discovered

"The world exists for the education of each person."
– Ralph Waldo Emerson

You are about to learn of a power that can only be called Divine. It permeates every ounce of energy in the universe and determines every detail of human life. The whole universe and everything in it operates using this awesome power. Upon discovering this power, a sense of wonder awakens within you.

The discovery of this power has to be the wildest thing any human being has ever discovered. Its utilization can lead to life without limits. You are going to learn how to maximize every aspect of your life—but first; you must deal with a belief that can block your ability to experience this unbelievable power. Let me assure you, life was originally created without limitations. The limitations we experience are self-imposed. As we go beyond our limited perspective of life, we can begin to envision what our lives might possibly become. How would you like to wake up every morning knowing you have the master key to life? You can be in control of your own destiny as you live the life you were created to live—a life without limitations.

My first encounter with this power came through a systematic study of

Metaphysics. I began to see that certain universal laws apply to all aspects of life. I noted by viewing parts of things I could envision and grasp the nature of the whole. I noticed that every moment of life instructs and wisdom is infused in the minute replicas of the whole. As Ralph Waldo Emerson wrote, "The world exists for the education of each person."[1] Looking beyond this entire material world, I discovered the spiritual world. It was evident that a Supreme Intelligence created everything and put it into place. Here is how I believe it all happened.

A Supreme Intelligence simply thought things into existence. The Creator thought of Light and said, "Let there be light" and the light appeared. Just imagine a Divine mind that simply thinks about things and calls them into existence—including humankind. This Divine Being becomes a part of everything it creates by breathing into them the energy of life. It is in everything. We witness it in an acorn that turns into a mighty oak tree. We see it in the limitless grains of sand on the seashore. We see it in the unlimited possibilities of scientific discovery. It gives everything, including you, unlimited power. If you know how this power works, you can have anything you want. You'll live a life without limits.

For centuries, only a few humans have known of this power, and those who used it experienced miracle after miracle. Their lives were limitless. The greatest example was Jesus of Nazareth. Jesus is known to Christians as the Son of God and to other religions as a great prophet and teacher. He healed people and performed many miracles. Using this incredible power, he conquered even death. Jesus constantly used this inner power that came directly from the Divine Creator.

Let's look closely at our world. Most people are not getting out of life all they deserve. You probably know people who work hard, but it seems they are just going through the motions—seemingly stuck in the "same old, same old." They are making no progress. Life is passing them by. They search for a better life but never seem to find it. They don't realize that inside them is a Divine Power that will enable them to achieve whatever they desire. Let's stop for a moment and ask, what do most people desire?

- Improved self-esteem
- Empowering self-confidence
- Boldness projected outward from inner feelings of self-worth

- The ability to work toward life's goals and accomplish them
- Efficient action that produces overwhelming success and results
- Free and full communication
- The feeling that they are connected to a Divine Being
- Personal control of one's destiny instead of being at the mercy of one's feelings and whims.

We all want a life without limits, wouldn't you agree? As a counselor, I have heard many people say it would be wonderful to:

- Awake each day feeling calm, positive, and filled with enthusiasm
- Feel mentally strong and emotionally energetic
- Find one's true place in the world
- Overcome tendencies that limit, block, and sabotage oneself

People are searching for something that will give them a life without limits. As you continue to read, I'll tell you how you can discover what you've been searching for. I'll show you how to go inside your mind and spirit and tap an awesome God-given power, a power that will assist you in meeting your every need.

If I told you that you could achieve everything you desire and live a prosperous life without limits, would you be interested? If your answer is yes, keep reading. I will tell you of four principles, the understanding of which will lead to a power that will enable you to live a life without limits. These four universal laws have been taught by the world's greatest minds: Jesus, Buddha, Mohammed, Confucius, Aristotle, Plato, and Emerson just to mention a few. By understanding these laws, great minds throughout all ages have gone beyond limitations. They've discovered a life originally created by a loving Creator whose desire is to see people live abundantly.

Let's examine each of these four laws to see how they work. The first law is **THERE IS AN INNER POWER WITHIN THAT CAN FREE YOU FROM ALL LIMITATIONS.** With this power, all outer limiting circumstances can be changed. This inner power is a power that is limitless, a power that simply has no limitations.

Once you get beyond the idea of limitations and believe in this awesome power, you can learn to control your thoughts and refuse to allow fear to enter your mind. Fear is the natural consequence of belief in limitations. This is why Jesus of Nazareth taught those around him to "fear not." There is no reason to fear anything when you possess this awesome, inner power. By learning to take control of your thoughts, you can have anything you desire. There is no limit to the good things that can come into your life.

The second fundamental law is **YOU MUST BELIEVE.** The power we're discussing will not work if you do not believe. For centuries, great teachers have told us "It is done unto you as you believe." Everything is based on belief. Everything in the universe was created by Divine belief. One thing we know for certain—anything you see or will ever see is a result of belief.

Historically, this Law of Belief has been used by only a few who chose to use it to discover new science, new art, and new philosophies. In fact, all new knowledge is a direct result of belief.

Tennyson wrote, "It is time for us to dip into the future as far as human eyes can see, See the vision of the world and all the wonders that would be…."[2] New technologies, new discoveries, and new inventions are all a result of belief. They had to believe in it, see it in their imagination, and then they could create it. Everything that exists is a result of belief.

The third fundamental law is **YOU MUST LEARN TO CONTROL YOUR THOUGHTS.** Why? Because your thoughts control your world. Your thoughts determine your destiny. "As a man thinks, so is he." All world religions reiterate that statement over and over again in many different languages to teach people the awesome power of thought. The thoughts in our mind are so powerful, everything gets expressed through them. Every living soul can awaken to this awesome power of mind. As Milton wrote in *Paradise Lost*, "The mind is its own place and in itself can make a heaven of hell, a hell of heaven."[3] The thoughts in your mind can create anything. Now listen closely—by taking control of your thoughts, you can create a life without limits. If you fail to take control of your thoughts, it will be anybody's guess what you will create.

Look around you. Countless millions are living in a heaven of opportunity, but they have no control of the outer circumstances of their lives because they have failed to take control of their thoughts. They are not taking responsibility for their thoughts, thereby facing a life of uncontrolled circumstances. They have opportunities for thoughts of love, yet they have thoughts of hate; opportunities for thoughts of success, yet they think thoughts of failure; opportunities to think of riches, yet they are thinking poverty.

In every walk of life you see them. You see their bitterness, their desolate expression, their sad eyes, and listless hands. They have condemned themselves to a life of limitations. They are just not mentally prepared to live. The thoughts that go through their minds daily are often random.

As Shakespeare wrote, "All things are ready if our minds be so."[4] But your mind is not ready until you have learned to control your thoughts. You are powerless to take control of your life until you control your thoughts. Opportunity after opportunity will pass before you because you are not in control of your thoughts.

Your mind is your most powerful possession, but its amazing power will never be yours unless you take control of it, understand it, and learn how to use it. This is not rocket science. Any average person can understand the simple workings of the mind and use this knowledge to enhance life as they learn to control their every thought.

Here are some things you need to know. We only have one mind that is an individualized part of one universal mind. Your mind has two important levels: the conscious level referred to as the rational level and the subconscious level often called the irrational level. The subconscious level stores all kinds of information that gets acted upon, while the conscious level deals with only what's happening to you at the present moment. Your subconscious is constantly working on your mental thoughts to make things happen. Throughout the remainder of this book, when I refer to the conscious mind and the subconscious mind, I'm not suggesting we have two minds but two parts that function as one individualized mind.

What I am about to share with you is one of the greatest secrets of all ages. Whatever you impress in your subconscious mind gets expressed in your outer life because your subconscious mind is connected to a cosmic mind that creates everything. This cosmic mind is constantly creating things.

Things appear in your outer world through a process called "manifestation". Once your subconscious mind accepts an idea, it begins to execute it. The subconscious mind, unlike the conscious mind, doesn't distinguish between what's good for you and what's bad for you. It makes no moral distinctions. In the Gospel According to Saint Matthew, this is what the biblical writer has in mind when he says, "It rains on the just and the unjust alike" (Matthew 5:45).

Therefore, as you work to control your thoughts, let go of any unwanted thoughts: thoughts of fear, worry, hatred, revenge, and so on. Just let them go. Let go of any thoughts that might bring you harm, and instead, intentionally hold on to thoughts that will enhance your life and the lives of others. Focus on thoughts of health, peace, happiness, prosperity, and peace of mind. Consistently impress good thoughts into your subconscious mind and your life will start to change.

Your subconscious mind doesn't reason like your conscious mind. It has no ability to dispute whatever you feed it. It will work tirelessly to manifest whatever you supply it. A remarkable example of this can be seen in the Hebrew Bible. A man named Job, a most impeccable character, faced hardship after hardship because of fearful thoughts. His whole life just crumbled into nothingness. He lost family, possessions, and on top of all this, he lost his health. Job remarked, "All that I feared has come upon me" (Job 3:25).

Never focus on thoughts of fear. Think on things that you desire. Think thoughts of peace, joy, freedom, courage, and happiness. Supply your subconscious mind with good thoughts and watch what happens. You'll be elated and overjoyed as good things start happening to you.

As your limitations disappear, you'll start living free of limitations—the way you were created to live. Surely no one in their right mind could believe that a Divine Creator would create people to face life with all kinds of limitations. It just seems reasonable that the Creator's desire is for us to live abundantly.

When some people hear this, they do not believe it. They think humans can never be free of limitation. They feel the best we can do is to put up with life the way it is. Old ideas die hard, but die they must to make room for new ideas. The only limits any of us have concerning life are the limits we impose on ourselves.

You can have a wonderful life by taking charge of your thoughts and "playing your cards right". Surely you've noticed some people start out in life with every advantage, but they play their hand so badly they end up with a very limited existence. Others appear to receive the poorest hand; but by taking responsibility, by disciplining their thoughts, and playing their hand successfully, their life has no limits. You can play your cards however you wish. Just be sure your thinking is constructive. Strive to be a role model for others since you want them to succeed, also.

This brings us to the fourth fundamental law: **EMANCIPATE YOURSELF FROM NEGATIVE THOUGHTS BY REPLACING ANY NEGATIVE THOUGHT WITH A POSITIVE ONE.** We all suffer from negative thoughts suggested to us by a cynical world. We can easily be influenced and misled by the cynicism of our day. Societal consciousness can contaminate our minds with conflicting opinions concerning limitations. Pay no attention to conflicting opinions. Here is the truth of the matter. We are born into a world created by a Divine Power that has no limitations. Unfortunately, from a child on, we are taught limitations. We are saturated with them day after day.

Your lower self will consistently tell you that you were born to live with limitations and you must accept them. Fortunately, your higher self is working to bring you to the realization that you were created to live beyond limitations. Each day as you follow your higher consciousness, you will find fewer and fewer limitations.

In Chapter Two, you will learn how to get in touch with your higher self.

CHAPTER 2

Moving Toward a Higher Consciousness

From time to time, a "still, small voice" whispers in our ear informing us that the Divine Intelligence of the universe has something to say. Often, the voice is hard to hear because of constant confusion on the outside.

What if I told you how you could block out constant confusion and hear this small voice loud and clear by focusing on what's going on inside of yourself rather than outside? Would you believe by paying attention to what's going on inside you can experience greater awareness? It is the first step toward a higher consciousness and the development of peace of mind.

Peace of mind comes as you screen out the outer world and focus on your inner world. With peace of mind, you can overcome the dissonance and confusion of the outer world. With peace of mind, you can think objectively about the world—a world that looks terrible but really isn't all that bad. Peace of mind allows you to get a handle on emotions that try to control your thoughts, thereby enabling you to act from a position of self-mastery, consequently getting in touch with your higher self. The reason for moving to a higher consciousness is that your simple consciousness does not have self-awareness. We see simple consciousness functioning in most animals whose daily desire is directed toward finding food, mating, and avoiding enemies—the things they do through instinct. Unlike the animal kingdom, Homo sapiens evolve from a state of simple consciousness to self-consciousness. Our consciousness has expanded itself through the formation of a more highly-developed human brain that has the potential for self-consciousness and reflective thought. The world is a training ground for developing our human consciousness as the Divine Creator of the universe calls us to a higher consciousness.

As we develop a higher consciousness, we start asking the essential question of life: What is my purpose in being? The unfolding of our purpose leads to a higher state of consciousness. The highest achievement of humanity is the triumph of rationality—the ability to reason and act logically, to create, and to plan for the future by living out our reason for being.

The only thing that can get in our way is our inability to handle our emotions constructively. To live up to what we know is our true purpose will take courage and vision, but with courage and vision we can become incredible human beings. People will automatically be attracted to us. They will want to be part of our lives.

They will often try to tell us what's best for us. Before taking their advice, take a long, hard look at what they've done with their own lives. Only on rare occasions will other people know what's best for us. After listening to the advice of others, be polite; but follow your own consciousness. Anytime you find yourself doubtful and confused, you can make course corrections by listening to your inner still, small voice.

The next problem you'll encounter is dealing with your own internal critic. We've all been subjected to a negative, critical environment; some of which has entered our conscious and has sunk into our subconscious mind.

As you deal with your internal critic, constantly think of yourself as you would be at your best. Behave and act today as if you've achieved a higher consciousness. You must do this for two reasons: (1) you have to believe in yourself to discover the person you were meant to be; (2) most people will take you at your own estimation of yourself. Whatever you believe about yourself will get communicated to the outside world by your actions, your words, your attitude, and your feelings. Believe it or not, others make decisions about who you are based on what you think of yourself.

The path to your best self is rarely straight. Your path will zigzag all over the place, but don't panic. Your still, small voice will guide you. You will learn from your mistakes as you keep going forward. This is what's called "failing forward." You can learn from your failure and move forward. No one gets life right 100% of the time.

Edison, the inventor of the electric light bulb, worked on that invention for a long time. When asked by one of his friends about his failure to perfect the invention, Edison remarked, "I haven't failed. I just know 999 ways that will not work."[5] He eventually invented that electric light bulb after more than 10,000 failures.

The reason history repeats itself is we do not learn from our mistakes the first time. However, you must refrain from kicking yourself or criticizing yourself. Talk to yourself in an encouraging voice. There is nothing as discouraging as self-criticism. Beating up on yourself will get you nowhere. When you fall flat on your face, pick yourself up! Falling on your face is no real disaster, but failing to get up is. If you pick yourself up after a defeat, you build self-confidence, self-esteem, and endurance.

If you doubt what I'm saying, observe children whose parents have protected them from the consequences of their actions. When we are not allowed to face the natural and logical consequences, we do not develop self-confidence. We become dependent.

All of us know persons in their thirties who still live with their parents. They may not have developed self-esteem due to the fact that their parents haven't allowed them to learn from their mistakes. Learning to correct our mistakes produces tremendous self-esteem.

By overcoming our problems, we forge ahead with added confidence to live life to the fullest, often developing a winning personality. Those who are protected from consequences develop abnormal personalities. They are often underdeveloped mentally and emotionally. As the old expression goes, "The lights are on and nobody's home." Most of these people are slaves to abnormal patterns of thinking, often saying they can't change. They are locked into a discouraged way of thinking; hence feeling tomorrow isn't going to get any better than today.

When the great architect Frank Lloyd Wright was asked which one of his designs was his favorite, without hesitation he responded, "My next one."[6] When you have confidence in yourself, you are excited about a better tomorrow, and the entire world awaits your next adventure.

With a higher consciousness, you place your head on your pillow at night at peace with yourself and with the whole world. Your heart is full of faith, and you cannot imagine not having a better tomorrow. The Divine

Creator is directing your life and you are playing the starring role. Like the Christ of Judea, you go about confidently doing good and helping others to overcome their mistakes. People who are confident learn from their failures. They overcome their mistakes and move on to a better, higher self. There is a motivating desire to move forward to a higher consciousness.

As you move to a higher consciousness, you will recognize you have a life purpose to fulfill. You can find satisfaction doing many things, but sooner or later you will have to do what you are meant to do. Listen to your still, small voice within as it tells you to be all you can be. The world needs your contributions. No one else can give to the world what you have to give. You are gifted and special. No other human being is exactly like you. You must realize who you really are and discover your own gifts because your gifts are needed. You are different. Every snowflake is different, every grain of sand on the seashore is different, and every tree, every rock, and every child has its own uniqueness. You must find out what your mission is. It isn't easy. It's a struggle that may take days, months, years, even decades. However, great people of all generations have endured this struggle. History is full of examples. Jesus of Nazareth spent forty days in the wilderness discovering his mission to humankind.

Saul of Tarsus went to Arabia for three years before he figured out what he was called to do. Moses had to go into the wilderness for 40+ years to discover who he was. Nobody said it is easy. It is certainly not for the faint of heart. However, if you are willing to endure, you can discover a higher consciousness and discover your mission in life. You'll get in touch with the person you were meant to be.

In Chapter Three, you'll learn how to put your higher consciousness to work to change your outer world by changing your inner thoughts. You'll learn that your thoughts do indeed create things.

CHAPTER 3

Change Your Outer World by Changing Your Inner Thoughts

"The oak sleeps in the acorn" –Unknown

Thus far you have learned that thoughts which occupy your mind and the ideas that are embedded in your heart determine your destiny. You are no doubt beginning to realize that the thoughts most held in the inner mind will always be manifested in your outer world. You are intelligent enough to know the life you are now living was created by your past thoughts. Imagine what it would be like if you could change your outer world by changing your inner thoughts—you can!

Many world-renown people have used the incredible secret I'm sharing with you. They learned that by changing their thoughts they could change their world. They came to the conclusion that life was pliable. The outer circumstances of your life are created by your thoughts, feelings, and attitudes. Most people want to be happy and healthy, but few realize a healthy body grows out of a happy mind. Our thoughts and ideas constitute our beliefs.

Everything we experience is directly related to our beliefs! Belief is the most powerful force in the universe, so powerful that it can manifest for us whatever we desire. Many people just simply aren't aware of the tremendous power of belief.

By exercising the Law of Belief—**BE IT DONE UNTO YOU AS YOU BELIEVE**—you can start manifesting things. To manifest is to show forth, to bring into being, or to make evident. Everything you see—plants, animals, humans, every visible thing—is a manifestation. As you make conscious use of the Law of Belief, plant an idea in mind and watch it grow into visible form, you are witnessing a manifestation as a child of the Creator. You, too, can manifest things into existence as you believe and apply the Law of Belief. Intelligent people of every generation have used this amazing power. They realize belief can produce anything that we need in life. Great religious teachers of all generations have told us, "It is done unto you as you believe." With belief, there is a power within that creates something without. It works perfectly every time. Your dominant belief will always be accepted by your subconscious mind which, in turn, works to manifest your belief in your external world. Once a belief is accepted subconsciously, your subconscious mind starts to work to make it happen. People throughout history have been able to do impossible things simply by knowing this incredible secret.

By now, you're beginning to realize how important belief is. Would you believe whatever you hold in your mind will show on your face? Your face is a billboard that advertises what's going on in your mind. Many of you remember as a child, you would simply walk into a room and your mother would take one look at you and say accusingly, "What have you been doing?" All she had to do was look at your face. As people mature to adulthood, they think they can hide their thoughts from others. Ninety-nine percent of the time, they are only fooling themselves. All of our past and present thoughts show on our face in some way. Abraham Lincoln is reported to have said, "You are not responsible for the face you were born with, but by the time you reach fifty years old, you are responsible for everything that shows on your face." You cannot hide your feelings because you cannot hide your thoughts.

Some have suggested that in the afterlife people communicate by reading each other's thoughts. Scary, isn't it? One mischievous look would prompt someone to ask, "What is he up to? What is she trying to hide? What has he done?" Everyone knows you cannot hide anything from the most important person in the world—you. Your facial expression will always match your inner thoughts no matter what kind of façade you try to put on. When you change your thoughts, your outer appearance will also change. This can be really good news if you are trying to clean up your act.

Presently, in your subconscious mind you have an accumulation of all kinds of past thoughts. Replacing some of these thoughts with healthier thoughts can enhance your life tremendously. You can change thoughts of fear to thoughts of courage. You can replace worry with peace of mind. You can let go of past difficulties that have held you back. You can consciously realize every minute of every day your thoughts can be guided by love and inspired by truth. Just think—thoughts of uncontrolled anger and rage as well as negative thoughts about yourself or others can be replaced with unconditional thoughts of love. You can replace rage with quietness and peace, anger with love, and thoughts of retaliation with thoughts of reconciliation. You can become a newer and healthier you. You can direct human thoughts much as an electrician directs the power of electricity.

By revamping your thoughts, you can change your life. Healthier thinking will bring all kinds of good things your way. Deciding to engage in healthy thinking is one of the most important decisions you will ever make.

Start now to dismiss unhealthy thoughts that come into your mind. Simply let them go and they will not affect you. When friends approach you with negative talk, be polite and let them talk. Don't waste energy trying to shut them up. Simply let go of their unhealthy contribution, wish them well, and continue to imagine your life changing in the direction you wish to go.

Picture yourself changing the direction of your life. It's only natural that old ways engrained deeply in your personality will resist your new way of life. Just keep your thoughts moving in a new positive direction. By taking control of your thoughts, you're playing a new game called "Change your life." You are engaging in the most productive behavior you have ever imagined. You are moving forward to a limitless life as you liberate yourself of old, unhealthy ways.

Liberation requires a great deal of disciplined thinking. The amazing fact is that by living an orderly life with calmness and tranquility, you can train your mind to function on a much higher level. You will be amazed at what you can accomplish. You will learn to order your thoughts and thus order your life. Your whole life will improve as you learn to use your mind properly. Your health, your relationships, and your financial picture will definitely improve. Little by little, as you manifest the life you desire, your family and friends will be amazed at the change that comes over you. They will be astonished as you come out of your troubles, out of your anxiety, out of your pain, and out of your very limited existence. They will marvel at how you've changed. Don't be surprised! They will want to know your secret.

Now I would like to help you experience something. Look at the world around you. Too many people are living lives of quiet desperation, thinking that whatever they do doesn't matter. What they need is a new life. They need a new philosophy of living and thinking. William James, a nineteenth century philosopher, believed that thoughts are valuable only to the extent that they have practical consequences in human experience.[7] In other words, the function of thought is to guide action. Every person lives in a world made for themselves by their own thoughts. Take control of your thoughts and you'll take control of your world. I've just told you something worth a trillion times the cost of this book. Please apply this to your life and witness what happens. You can change your life forever. I challenge you to be all you were meant to be. You were created with a purpose, and that purpose is to utilize all the potential you've been given.

Promise yourself today that you will begin the process of becoming all you can be. There is tremendous potential in you. Inside the acorn there is an oak that is just waiting to be. Inside the little acorn there are all kinds of things going on, all leading to a process of unfolding growth. One day the acorn will be a giant oak just as it was meant to be.

Inside the egg there is a bird growing, breathing, just waiting to be free. Inside every human being there is a higher self waiting to be. The new self, unlike the old one, is not limited. To discover your true self is to discover a limitless life. Just imagine what that would mean for you! It would mean discovering a higher consciousness, your true Spiritual Self. It's time we talked about your true Spiritual Self and what it means to be spiritual.

CHAPTER 4

What Does it Mean to be Spiritual?

One must be spiritual to experience life without limitations.

When you're spiritual, fear and anxieties give way to faith. Doubts give way to trust. Anger and hate get lost somewhere in goodwill. Guilt loses its bitterness in reconciling love. To be spiritual is to be in the process of becoming the person you were meant to be. It is to be molded by an inner power that is Divine.

Many people are not aware of the inner spiritual power that operates within each of us. In fact, this power is not limited to humans. It is in every living thing. Spiritual power is the power behind all life, expressing itself in everything. It is the energy behind all constructive thought.

This spiritual power works in humans to enhance intelligence, health, happiness, peace, prosperity, supply, and activity. It works to guide us to a complete and perfect life. It has no limitations except the limitations we impose on it.

The world would suddenly be at peace if everyone chose to follow their inner, spiritual power. Many of today's problems are the result of a spiritual crisis. This is due in part to our tendency to substitute religion for spirituality. Every man's religion seems good to him. While religion is a set or institutional system of religious attitudes, beliefs, and practices, spirituality is the quality or state of being sensitive to the Spirit. To be spiritual is to be directed by an inner, spiritual power that works to resurrect broken humanity. When you understand what it means to be spiritual, you get excited about life, realizing that being spiritual can lead to a life without limitations. The more spiritual you are the more life you enjoy and the better you are for yourself and others. Spiritual people are filled with love; therefore, they act out of love. They love their neighbors and they love themselves. They know there can be no true spiritual growth without the highest love for self and neighbors. They retire at night in peace knowing that no harm can come to a loving spirit. They are in a constant process of spiritual evolution. They arise every morning renewed in body and in mind with a brighter outlook, a happier expectation, and a glowing countenance. Spiritual people are enlightened. They know the highest love for self benefits others as well as themselves. They look upon all with love, condemning none, and bless even their enemies. They do not allow the world's competition and bitterness to shake their love for themselves or others. They trust the Divine Power immanent in the universe as they grow spiritually. Deep within, they know something is working within them and they can truthfully say they are being led by the Spirit.

The Spirit will always be expressive if you let it express itself through you. You will discover that out of your greatest difficulty, the Spirit will give you your greatest direction. As the Spirit leads, you'll discover real life, and you will start to feel better about living. You will experience what it feels like to really feel good. You will start to see the living Power in all things because it is the energy in all things.

True spirituality does not mean giving up personal pleasures or being resigned to whatever happens in life. Spiritual people know life is filled with good things. As you realize there is a lot of good in the world, you'll be glad to take the high road. You will realize the Spirit can make only good things happen. Historically, we've had people who were so connected to this Divine, inner Spirit that they, too, could make good things happen. They were often able to manifest things. If you are interested in a deeper spiritual experience, let's talk!

A deeper spiritual life comes by realizing the constant presence of an inner Spirit and relying on it. Here is how it works. Imagine yourself under Divine guidance relying on the Divine Spirit to empower you. You are determined to give up all corrupt (evil) thoughts and actions. This is necessary because the inner, spiritual power in you is only good. It cannot recognize evil because evil doesn't exist in the spiritual world. You want only the good in life anyway. I don't encounter any normal people wanting to hold on to corruption or evil.

Are you ready to start the journey toward a deeper spiritual life? If so, when you start, do not allow anyone to get you off track. If something happens and you do get off track, don't lose any time getting back on. You can trust your inner spiritual power at all times, in all places, and under all circumstances.

This is exciting because every day you are in the process of developing. You will want to be flexible. Your life is filled with good changes. Beware of prior conditioning and rigidity because it can lead to a broken spirit. Follow the Spirit's guidance. Don't resist. Resistance leads to frustration and defeat. Flexibility is essential to spiritual development.

As you awaken to the Divine Spirit within you, your subconscious mind will resist because old, corrupt, evil, and negative data contained within will not want to be replaced. The stuff I'm referring to is what causes you nightmares. You will have those times when materials come out to the conscious mind. They are usually not pleasant, but when they surface, hang in there. Once you cleanse your subconscious, your life without limitations will begin. You will lose a part of what it means to be human as you find what it means to be Divine. You will start to use the good resources your inner spirit has stored within your subconscious mind. There is simply no limit to what you have stored there since your subconscious is a well of information. It knows everything. It is your connection to God and God is not limited.

Outstanding minds of all generations have drawn from their subconscious mind. It gave them ideas, skills, information, and answers to all of life's most perplexing problems. It is your book of life. Literally every thought, action, idea, opinion, theory, and event of your life are stored there. Every moment in time is stored within your subconscious. You know by now that once your conscious mind accepts a thought completely it is automatically transferred to your subconscious. This stored information is then made manifest in your everyday life and existence. Your subconscious mind is, without question, the world's largest storage tank. And, furthermore, it is completely subjective. It accepts without question whatever you allow to sink into it. As Emerson wrote, "Man is what he thinks about all day long."[8] Now you know why I insist that you think only good thoughts.

Your thoughts, behaviors, and spoken words will affect your

conscious and subconscious mind, thus allowing your subconscious mind to manifest things in your outer life. As you consciously think about good things, good things will seep into your subconscious mind. If your thoughts are of good things, greater amounts of endorphins including serotonin will be released by your brain into your bloodstream, giving you a spiritual sense of aliveness and contentment. You will feel better than you have ever felt before.

Now let me get technical. Whatever gets impressed in your subconscious mind gets expressed in time in the outer experiences of your life. This is why I'm suggesting you allow the Spirit to guide you. When you are in harmony with the great forward movement of the Spirit, there is nothing that can hinder your advancement. If you oppose it, somewhere along the line it will crush you.

William James refers to the subconscious mind as the power to move the world.[9] Spiritual giants and illumined seers have used their inner spiritual power to accomplish great things. Their experiences have taught them the world within creates the world without. All you need to do is believe in your inner spiritual power and use it. Since the beginning of time, this Divine Spiritual Power has been the Creative Force behind everything. It is ever operative, ever creating, eternally making something out of matter. A spiritual person simply looks beyond the material world and sees this incredible inner power, an inner spiritual power that transcends all limitations, a power that manifests and creates constantly through your subconscious mind. To experience this power, use the following conscious mind-focusing exercise. Pick out three or four one-line positive affirmations to follow. Use short sentences such as:

- I have peace of mind.
- I am a spiritual person.
- I am healthy.
- I am filled with happiness.

Use these or other creative one-liners to visualize yourself as a spiritual person who has peace of mind, happiness, and health. Say your affirmations of choice three to four times a day for twenty-one days to allow your conscious affirmations to seep into your subconscious and then evaluate. You will discover a delightful difference in your attitude, feeling, and mental state.

As you are doing the aforementioned exercise, after three or four days add the following nightly exercise. This is what I call a Conscious to Subconscious Mind Exercise. At bedtime just prior to sleep, as you relax release thoughts, ideas, and impressions that you wish to manifest into your subconscious mind. Make sure you are relaxed and comfortable. Develop a memorized list of the things you desire. Visualize them as having already happened. Practice this each night for two weeks and then evaluate. You will be amazed at how many of the things you have visualized have already occurred in your outer life.

Here is how this works. Quantum spirituality shows us that the quantum mechanics we already possess provides us with a connection between the human mind and the cosmos. The theology behind this view of spirituality is that God has created a way to interact with humanity without violating natural laws. The intent behind this quantum spirituality is we make our own way. This is a renewal of an old paradigm in our understanding of reality. With your human mind, you have the ability to tune into the "cosmic mind" that pervades the universe. Upon recognizing your ability to tune into the "cosmic mind," you recognize how you can relate to the cosmic consciousness. This spiritual insight enables you to experience true spiritual growth.

As you receive information through your senses, you become what you think about and focus upon since your subconscious will faithfully manifest the habitual thoughts of your conscious mind. To live a life without limitations, you must choose to live as the Spirit directs since the Spirit has no limitations. Be true to your own spirit, make your own decisions. If you try to live to please others, you will lose your way. Your success depends on you being led by the Spirit. Spiritual insight is the only true insight. Your goal is to be led to your highest spiritual self or self-realization. The art of self-realization is the art of adjusting your individual mind to the universal mind, the art of becoming a channel for the flow of wisdom. By doing this, you will get to know your real self. You will become conscious of the ground of all being. Consciousness is the primary reality. All things are made of the energy of consciousness.

As soon as the masses discover that consciousness (Spirit) and not matter is the link that connects us to each other and the world, our views of war and peace, environmental pollution, social justice, religious values, and all other human endeavors will change radically for the better.

Listen closely to what I'm about to say! Everything including matter exists and is manipulated by consciousness!

If you are not enlightened, please consider allowing the Divine Spirit to lead you. Until you do, you will have nothing in life but limitation after limitation. Simply stated, if your mind is of a lower order occupied by worldly matters, you will encounter limitation after limitation. If your mind is of a higher order, you can move beyond limitations.

The good news is you can overcome all limitations by consciously changing your thoughts. You can enter a new kingdom with a life beyond limitations. You can rise above evil and weakness. You do not have to be a slave to circumstances. You do not need to be forever wallowing in a bog of doubt. You do not need to be drawn continually into the quicksand of fear. You do not need to be blown about by the winds of society. If I'm describing you and you desire to change, here is how you can change your life.

1. Learn to focus your thoughts on the good things you desire by cultivating calmness and repose in your daily thoughts. Focus on calmness, peace, and harmony. The minute anxiety enters your mind, push it out. Blaise Pascal (1623-1662) said, "All of our problems are derived from not being able to sit quietly in a room alone."[10] We should not be surprised that we have trouble with silence. The world puts little or no value on silence. You must learn how to be silent. You must learn to use the most powerful silent force in the universe—the thought force that is generated by your mind. Once a person enters the possession of this force, the whole trend of life advances.

2. You must realize the outward events in your life will always parallel your inner thoughts (your inner Spirit). An example of how this works can be seen by reading the Hebrew prophets of the Old Testament. They related national disasters to the dominant thought currents that penetrated their nation. They believed national events were simply the working out of the psychic fear of the nation; wars, plagues, and famine were consequences of wrong-directed thought forces, the culminating points at which destruction steps in as the agent of the Law.

3. The events of the universe grow out of thought matter. It's impossible to deny that everything is created in thought. The architect draws up plans created in thought to build a dream home. As the thoughts of the builder change along the way, the plans change.

4. Your thoughts build what you manifest. When they are directed in harmony with an overriding law, you are building something, but when your thoughts run counter to natural law, they are destructive. Therefore, be sure to think thoughts of peace, happiness, and goodwill. Apply the subtle force of your power of thought to yourself as well as everyone else. Your inner spiritual power will enable you to transform your life as your good thoughts quickly become actualized in your outer circumstances. Hold yourself open to the Infinite Mind, the all-powerful force that wishes good for the world. Join in the music of joy. Like a bird, you do not make your own music. Hold yourself open to the Infinite Mind and that mind will pour the music through you. This is how you receive spiritual inspiration and power.

In the next chapter, we'll discuss the awakened life.

CHAPTER 5

The Steps to an Awakened Life

The world is not awake. Look around you.

We live in a world that is filled with knowledge; knowledge that can be used to achieve an awakened life. We know everything about everything. However, we know a lot of things that just aren't true. We carry on our backs a shell like a turtle made up of lies that we've been led to believe. Ridding ourselves of this shell is hard, emotional work. However, we must rid ourselves of this shell of lies to live an awakened life.

We are all infinite beings with intelligence, awareness, and infinite bliss. We are Godlike, but our God-likeness is buried under an almost impenetrable shell of distractions, assumptions, and self-defeating impulses that comprise our surface self. By and large, we are powerless until we rid ourselves of this shell and learn to control our thoughts. Controlling our thoughts is very difficult. So many thoughts go through our minds that it seems utterly impossible to control them. Things are just moving too fast.

In early frontier days, if you missed a stagecoach you simply settled down and waited for the next one. After all, there was no problem. They ran every six months. Now, if people miss one section of a revolving door, they complain their lives are out of control.

Our fast-paced society creates a lot of anxiety for all of us, making it difficult to control our thoughts. On top of all this, the average person has a deep reservoir of repressed anxiety stored in the subconscious mind. We have uncontrolled negative thoughts and emotions. If you could x-ray your subconscious, you would not believe the anxiety, frustration, hurt, jealousy, envy, and a host of other emotions stored there. Until you learn to process and deal with such emotions, your thoughts are going to be impossible to control.

Herein lies the problem. Life's important decisions come crashing in on you daily. Most people have reserved little time for contemplation, meditation, and inner reflection because they are just not in vogue. Consequently, most of us make life-changing decisions without inner consultation. Most people feel they don't have time to think about the consequences of their decisions.

Fifty years ago most people would contemplate, meditate, reflect, and ponder for days before making life-changing decisions. Now decisions are made instantly. We say times have changed. Times haven't changed—we have! It is no wonder we feel we have little control of our lives, and we are just going through the motions. We need to wake up. We need an awakened life to regain our power of choice.

Stop and think! What would happen if you took charge of your life and made decisions by going inside yourself to find answers? I can guarantee your life would change drastically. You would find tremendous solutions to your problems, and you would experience remarkable results. All you need to do is learn how to go inside your mind and ask your subconscious mind for answers.

Some of you are thinking, "I can't do that. I can't go inside. I don't know how to do that. Besides, people who do things like that are spooky, weird, spiritual types." Would you be less hesitant if I told you that everyone goes inside, everyone meditates? Even the most seemingly non-spiritual people meditate. I'll prove it to you.

Every year millions of people meditate deeply on the subject of sports without realizing that they are doing so. Something like this happens. John gets up early in the morning, picks up all the problems of life that he left behind while he was sleeping, puts on his clothes, eats breakfast, watches the news on television, turns to the Sports Channel and watches it for a few minutes. He becomes absorbed in what he is hearing and all other subjects fade out of his mind: home troubles, business troubles, politics, and other crises are all forgotten. He is lost in meditation. He criticizes the management of his favorite team that has lost. He thinks of changes that should have been made, and the next thing he knows it's time to go to work. This is first-class meditation on the subject of sports. John can come up with solutions to problems in his life in the same way he ponders the changes his favorite team should have made. He just needs to know how he can live an awakened life.

What if, instead of turning on the Sports Channel, John sat in a quiet place and learned to go inside himself for a while and control his thinking? What if he thought about things he desired? What if he had a problem and presented it to his subconscious mind and believed that his subconscious mind would provide an answer? He could find solutions to his most complicated problems. As we search for answers, our subconscious can supply the answers we are seeking. In fact, our subconscious mind knows everything. Believe it or not, the answers are already there in our subconscious minds. If we are patient, the answers we are seeking will always come. If we are impatient and give up because we are not getting an answer immediately, we will abort our request. We must be patient and believe the answer will come. As we believe, the answer will arrive.

Those who understand and apply what I've just revealed to you will enjoy amazing results. You can provide inventions, discoveries, and numerous other wonderful things to advance civilization in countless ways. All our experiences, events, conditions, and acts are produced by our subconscious mind.

Here is how it works. Thoughts and desires held over a period of time in our conscious mind will seep into the subconscious mind and manifest themselves in our outer world. Negative thoughts as well as positive thoughts will manifest. This is why you must let go of negative beliefs, opinions, superstitions, and fears that plague you and focus on positive desires and beliefs that will lead you closer and closer to an awakened life.

I began this chapter with these words: "The world is not awake...." When you start to see how you can be awakened to think constructively, you can make a difference in our world, you can take yourself out of the mass consciousness of the world and start your journey toward a higher level of consciousness.

Here is how to put into practice what I'm suggesting. Practice intentionally, filling your mind with concepts of harmony, health, peace, and goodwill; and miracles will start happening in your life. You will start to live an awakened life without limits. You will discover that by controlling your thoughts and imagination, you can create whatever you desire as you tap into the creativeness of your subconscious mind.

Great artists, writers, and musicians have used this method to tap into their subconscious mind to imagine, visualize and create the world's masterpieces. As Einstein said, "Imagination is more important than knowledge."[11] Your subconscious mind is filled with knowledge. It is far more knowledgeable than you've ever imagined. It is the creative, spiritual part of your mind; it is knowledgeable enough to function in both the mental and physical aspects of life. It takes care of your breathing, your digestion, and every other bodily function without any need for your conscious mind to intervene, and it will create for you whatever you think into it.

If you were forced to operate your body's functions without your subconscious mind, you would die a quick death. Granted, modern technology is incredible. The heart-lung machine used in open heart surgery is a miracle of the most advanced technology, but what it does is infinitely simpler than what your subconscious does twenty-four hours a day.

As you learn to control your thoughts, you will literally experience an awakened life.

In the next chapter, you'll discover how to live a magical life as you explore the secrets of those who lived magically.

CHAPTER 6

Life Becomes Cold When There is No Magic in It

Imagine walking through a cemetery and seeing a tombstone on which the epitaph reads, "Here lies one who lived a magical life." Your first thought is, "Wow! I wish I could have known this person." His life was so incredible others deemed it magical. You begin to contemplate what a magical life would look like as you think "Wow! I wish I knew his secret."

Wouldn't it be amazing if you could discover the secret of living a magical life? You can! As you examine how magical people live, you will discover what makes them magical. We've all known such people. We are so in awe of how they live, we generally pay little attention to what they are doing.

After researching several magical lives up close, I've discovered some amazing secrets that I want to share with you. First, I discovered magical people are living on all three planes of life: physical, spiritual, and intellectual.

Since we are all born into the physical plane of life, it often becomes so important to us that it becomes our number one priority at the neglect of the spiritual and intellectual planes of our lives. In fact, there are some who seem convinced that the physical is all there is. They have not discovered how much human evolution has progressed. Just one experience that goes beyond the physical and scratches the surface of the spiritual can alert you to its importance. Spiritually, you can get in touch with the great truths of the universe. As Albert Einstein stated in his credo, "What I Believe":

> *The most beautiful emotion we can experience is the mysterious. It is the fundamental emotion that stands at the cradle of all true art and science. He to whom this emotion is a stranger, who can no longer wonder and stand rapt in awe, is as good as dead, a snuffed-out candle. To sense that behind anything that can be experienced there is something that our minds cannot grasp, whose beauty and sublimity reaches us only indirectly: this is religiousness. In this sense, and in this sense only, I am a devoutly religious man.*[12]

This coming from a man many people considered to be an atheist. But in his writings it is clear that he recognized the existence of the spiritual plane. He knew that a spiritual experience offers first-hand knowledge of life and reality. You may have heard someone say, "I know how you feel." The truth is they don't know how you feel unless they have spiritually experienced what you are experiencing. Spiritually, you can never know peace until you've experienced it. You can never know truth until you've experienced it. You can be taught truth, but truth means nothing unless it becomes your truth.

If you haven't experienced the spiritual plane, you're missing much of life since so much of life exists on the spiritual plane. For instance, it is useless for a person with a troubled mind to ask for peace if he or she is living only on the physical plane. Peace exists on the spiritual plane. Peace comes only from within. When nations sign peace treaties on the physical plane, the peace they have long sought has already occurred on the spiritual plane. As nations sign a treaty, they only confirm what has already happened and promise to honor the spirit of what has transpired.

Life grows cold when one neglects the spiritual plane. The same is true intellectually. All human troubles are a result of intellectual ignorance. Our intellect is the foundation of everything. It helps us to know how to apply spiritual laws and principles. As we live on the spiritual plane, we have an open and receptive mind intellectually. This enables us to experience all the good that a limitless, creative, universal spirit may bring.

The old materialistic belief that we are a body with a spirit is replaced by the inspiring belief that we are a spirit with a body and an intellect. Our spiritual nature puts us in touch with our intellect (our mind) as the knowledge, wisdom, and thought processes of our mind create our world.

As we have established, life is meant to be lived on all three planes: physical, intellectual, and spiritual in order to achieve our fullest human potential. To live totally on the physical plane would be savage. To live only on the spiritual plane is to be a dreamer without a practical side, and if we live entirely on the intellectual plane, we become only an elitist robot without a body or spirit. Avoiding any of these three levels of existence renders one cold and lifeless. Our physical body is alive with unknown abilities, and it looks to the intellectual and spiritual aspects of our being for direction. For example, when a golfer says the game of golf is won or lost in his head, this is what he is referring to. The game is as much intellectual as it is physical and, I daresay, it has also become spiritual. Some golfers are on the course religiously every day. Playing golf has become almost sacred. Golfers will tell you they can worship God on the golf course as easily as they can in a church, synagogue, or mosque.

As stated previously, your physical body looks to the spiritual and intellectual aspects of your being as to how your life will be directed instead of leaving everything to fate. Each of us can decide how our life is to be directed instead of leaving everything to fate.

Now let's talk about the "how to" of living a magical life. Start by loving yourself. As Emerson said, "I the imperfect adore the Perfect; glorify the Creator in your body for you are a child of the Divine."[13] You must honor, respect, and love your "self" to honor, respect, and love others. If you do not love yourself, it is impossible to love others. It will also be impossible for others to love you.

If you are down on yourself, the energy you send out will communicate that you don't like yourself, and others will feel they shouldn't like you either. The way you feel about yourself will always come back on you. You'll be like the man who bought a new boomerang and killed himself trying to throw the old one away.

Self-criticism is the most destructive poison of all. It sinks deep into your subconscious mind and literally robs you of vitality, energy, and enthusiasm leaving you a wreck spiritually, intellectually, and physically. Practice loving yourself by imagining yourself at your best. Your image of yourself will eventually sink into your subconscious. Your subconscious will work to bring your best to fruition. Practice being positive. Focus your thought daily on what you want out of life, not on what you don't want.

Daily set some time aside to imagine yourself at your best and plan for optimal output. Devote time each day to engage your mind in constructive thinking; affirming and building yourself up. Avoid making excuses when things do not go right. Just pause for a moment and redirect yourself. Remember, no matter how desperate life becomes, you should never get down on yourself. If things are not as they should be, examine your thoughts. You may need to change your thinking. Your inner thoughts create your outer circumstances. If you change your thoughts, you can change your circumstances. Surrounding you is this tremendous energy field. This energy is either attractive energy or repulsive energy. If you love yourself and others and you are thinking incredible, constructive thoughts; you will have an abundance of attractive energy. Everyone will want to befriend you.

The mental atmosphere I have just referred to is known as an aura. Our aura is always determined by our subconscious. It varies in size and intensity and changes as your mentality changes. If you become very angry, your aura is filled with intense lightning. If you could see the aura of two very angry persons colliding, you would see sparks fly. We've all heard someone say the room was so tense you could feel sparks fly. This is why two angry people trying to communicate, results in little or no communication. An aura of anger, rage, or hatred will result in conflict, struggle, fight, or even war.

On the other hand; a calm, amiable, and friendly aura attracts people. It brings peace, penetrates the bonds of misunderstanding, and brings joy and peace to others. The Christ of Judea said, "Blessed are the peacemakers for they will be called "children of God" (Matthew 5:9, New Revised Standard Version). If you are living a magical life, your desire will always be to bring joy, peace, and hope to others. What I am suggesting is when you are around people for any length of time, they will start to feel the joy, the peace, and the hope you are feeling inside.

Now that you have some knowledge of how a magical life works, let's look at some ways to add magic to your days. I know you want to look upon the future with cheerful enthusiasm, a radiant belief in life, and a heartfelt belief in humanity. We all can become persons through whom the Divine Creator can work. We want to think on the good things of life, and we can, because the magical life is available to all who ask, believe, and receive. It's available to all who will use their minds in a constructive way and are actively thinking and manifesting good things. Why not make your thoughts productive?

We are thinking beings. We cannot stop thinking. We have approximately 60,000 thoughts a day.[14] Our subconscious mind receives our thoughts and starts to work on whatever we ask. As our conscious thoughts seep into our subconscious mind, our subconscious starts to manifest our thoughts. The subconscious mind will return to you what you ask or think into it. "It is done unto you as you believe." This is why belief is so important. If you don't believe in the power within you that causes all things to happen, it cannot and will not work for you. The Divine Creator is always ready to pour into your experience whatever you ask.

To push this principle a little further, the Law of Belief works when you can believe in things not seen. This is really what faith is all about. In other words, you must believe you will receive before things appear in your life. Your belief provides a receptive avenue for you to receive. Your task is to believe and never waiver no matter what happens.

As a consultant, I've had the opportunity to work with people on some huge projects. Upon completion of a project, the greatest compliment anyone can receive is: You helped us believe it was possible. At the point I was called in on projects, they often did not believe they could achieve their goals. I had to believe for them and help them believe they could do it. During the project, they gradually began to believe they could achieve their goals. By the end of the project, they saw the results of believing in themselves as they not only accomplished their goals but surpassed their expectations.

Never allow yourself to think limitations or failure. When failures come to mind, erase the idea from your mind. The reason for this exercise is quite obvious. If one believes in failure or feels he has failed previously, he will likely fail again. You can never live a magical life and believe in failure. Often someone will say to deny failure is not facing reality. If we deny failure, we're being dishonest with ourselves. My response is: the Creative Spirit that dwells in us never fails. The power of this Spirit supplies us with all the energy we need. The Spirit doesn't know failure. Don't you believe we can trust this Spirit? A constant supply of this Spirit flows through you to energize your talents and abilities; making your life rich, full, and abundant. You have only to recognize and receive this unlimited supply of energy. It is always there for the believer.

I challenge you to look upon life with radiant acceptance and receive all the energy you need. You can feel it flowing through you. Try this simple exercise for seven days, ten to fifteen minutes each day: Go to a quiet place. Close your eyes, quiet your mind, and feel positive thought energy flowing through you. Don't allow yourself to dwell on any negative thought energy. Each time you encounter a negative thought, replace it with a positive one. In a couple of days, you will find yourself beginning to experience the positive energy of life. You will start to feel an incredible power welling up inside you as your subconscious mind aligns itself with the Creative Mind of the universe. You will start to discover solutions to your current problems, you'll find joy appearing where sadness existed before, you'll discover the world truly *is* filled with joy, peace, and love and you'll start to feel that life is truly magical.

This little exercise will bring an unending supply of energy to you and give you confidence for tomorrow. You'll realize your best days are still ahead.

In the next chapter, we'll discuss how you can renew your life by renewing your mind.

CHAPTER 7

Renew Your Life by Renewing Your Mind

Since your life is controlled by your thoughts, managing your mind is of critical importance. Your mind makes it possible for you to discover your rightful place in the universe. It is the most powerful thing you possess. Properly used, it will supply you with everything you need to live a life without limits.

As previously stated, the key to unlocking the power of mind is belief. Therefore, you must understand belief to achieve your desires. The Law of Belief simply stated is: **IT IS DONE UNTO YOU AS YOU BELIEVE.** Belief starts with a specific thought in mind that continues to make itself known in consciousness until it sweeps into your subconscious mind. When it arrives, the subconscious mind starts to work on it immediately to bring it to fruition in the outer experiences of life. As the Bible says, "If you can believe, all things are possible to him that believes" (Mark 9:23, NRSV).

The Law of Belief works for things that will enhance your life as well as things that will harm it. The old saying "It rains on the just and the unjust alike" tells how the Law of Belief operates. It will deliver to you whatever you believe. Knowing this all-important fact, you may want to stop thinking about things that will harm you to avoid bringing harmful things into your life. Instead, think of good things to bring good things into your life, knowing your subconscious mind processes any request handed to it by your conscious mind.

By creating a blueprint for happiness and abundance, you can be confident that you are building an inner life that will create your heart's desire. With your subconscious mind assisting you, you will never be limited. You simply think thoughts into the Universal Spirit that creates and is unlimited as to what it can create. Remind yourself each day that constant thoughts seep gently into your subconscious which, in turn, starts to work to bring about whatever you are thinking. In three simple words: thoughts produce things.

Unfortunately, bad thoughts bring bad things into your life just as easily as good thoughts bring good things. Focus on controlling your thoughts and you can achieve whatever you desire.

As stated in a previous chapter, it is a proven fact that control of thoughts brings focus of mind, and focus of mind brings you whatever you desire. Some of you are saying that sounds too good to be true. There is an inner critic in each of us that insists that no one can control their thoughts. Don't listen to your inner critic. There is a way to control the 60,000+ thoughts per day that go through an average mind. Here is the secret. We have been given an inner power that will help us control our thoughts; and, with a little practice, we can become very proficient. In fact, controlling our thoughts can lead to happiness.

Do you know why some people are happy most of the time? They control their thoughts. They constantly think happy thoughts. This is why I'm an optimist. I learned if you want to be happy you have to think happy thoughts. You must think optimistically. Let me tell you how this works. A negative thought—any thought of failure, criticism, jealousy, trouble, or spite will severely limit your possibility for happiness. Negative thoughts start your subconscious mind to work on bringing negative things into your life—things you don't want. Down deep, most of you know what I'm saying is true. Your heart, your brain, and your spirit align themselves with this truth. Being negative will get you what you *don't* want! This is why I suggest you renew your life by renewing your mind.

Everyone knows life throws enough negative stuff at us daily to bury all of us in a short period of time. We hear all kinds of tragedy, calamity, and misfortune daily on the news. We read it in the newspapers and see it on televisions and computers. We hear it in conversations with friends and colleagues at work. Most of us experience enough negative stuff in one eight-hour day to bury us if we dwell on the negative.

So how do we survive? And how do we help others survive? Obviously, sharing our troubles is not going to help. We hear "misery loves company," and "like attracts like," but we're not going to help ourselves or others by discussing our personal misery.

To benefit yourself and others, you must remain optimistic. You can be an example for the weak by mirroring happiness, peace, and prosperity. By doing this, you'll attract others in large numbers. People are hungry for encouragement. Deep down, most people believe life is good. They want to believe they can have a better tomorrow. They long to have confidence in themselves, in life, and in others. Something deep within is calling us to a better life.

By remaining optimistic and trusting their inner power, anyone can transcend negativism and move forward to a better life. By thinking thoughts of harmony, goodwill, peace, and prosperity, one can have a happier life. By changing one's outlook on life, one can be empowered to overcome anything that is distressing. A good attitude about life in general will go a long way. We meet too many people who have a bad attitude. Some of you are thinking, "Okay, but how do I keep a good attitude when I constantly encounter those with a bad attitude?" You must do your own thinking. Other's thoughts can have no power over you unless you give them power over you.

Let's suppose someone with a bad attitude spreads lies about you. Of course, if you are normal, you are going to feel angry. But someone else's opinion of you should not change how you feel about yourself. You never allow others to manipulate your attitude about yourself or anyone else. You have the power to control your own thinking. When others say bad things about you, think good of them. Continue to be the marvelous person you really are. Think good thoughts of everyone. Follow the Golden Rule: **DO UNTO OTHERS AS YOU WOULD HAVE THEM DO UNTO YOU.** You will always win in the long run. As an old saying goes, "We can't keep the birds from flying over our heads, but we can keep them from building nests in our hair." Stay positive, keep thinking everything will turn out right and it will. Keep believing that most people are wonderful and most things are fundamentally right in your world and they *will* be. Some may say, "Isn't that just wishful thinking?" You bet it is, but isn't it sad that some people do not believe in wishful thinking? Webster Dictionary defines wishful as "to desire, want, request, hope, pray for, and look forward to." As a child, we learn to wish for things. We can pair wishful thinking with positive action and achieve any of our desires.

When I was twelve years old, I told my friend Gary that I was going to save up the money I made mowing lawns and buy a used car. Gary told me that was just wishful thinking. When I was fifteen, I had enough money to buy my first car. When Gary saw a 1955 Plymouth parked in my driveway, he changed his mind about wishful thinking. Throughout the ages, people have attracted millions of things into their lives by wishful thinking. If you don't believe in wishful thinking, you are simply cheating yourself. Don't ever stop wishing for the things you desire. Don't allow anyone to rain on your parade.

Remember this: no one is born with a bad attitude. No downcast person can ever be truly happy. We've all known people who really work at being unhappy. This type of person is characterized in this old American frontier adage: He would be unhappy if you hung him with a new rope! Unfortunately, some people have made it a habit to function only in their dysfunction. You don't want to be one of them. You'll be happier if you are positive, love life, love people, love what you do, and believe good things are coming your way each and every day.

Whenever life throws you a curve and the storms of life hit you, don't allow the storm to get inside of you. Someone has wisely said, "You measure a person's success by how much they bounce when they hit bottom." When you hit bottom, you want to bounce all the way back to the top.

It's true! Rebounding from a storm requires belief in a power greater than your own. You can trust the Infinite Power of the Universe. Place your confidence in this Universal Power and have no doubt. You can count on the presence of the Divine Creator.

Let's review. As you discover the presence of the Infinite Power of the universe, you will open up the channel through your subconscious for good things to come into your life. You will learn to count your blessings daily. You will stop rehashing old problems and difficulties. Practice four things daily:

1. Visualize the Divine Presence within you.
2. Cleanse your mind of all negative thoughts: anger, fear, resentment, and so on.
3. Forgive everyone who has injured you to avoid accumulating negative thoughts in the recesses of your subconscious mind.
4. Concentrate daily on the good things you desire.

Never allow your mind to get discouraged. We all have occasions when difficulties seem to occupy our minds for too long. We start thinking: "What's the use? I'll just give up." This kind of thinking does not help. On days like this, turn your thoughts to the things that are going right in your life. Focus on the things for which you are grateful. As you do this, more and more good things will come your way. Focus on the good things that come into your life. There is not a minute in any twenty-four hour period that doesn't contain some miracle.

All of us need to look upon life with radiant expression, cheerful enthusiasm, and receptive minds. Do not dwell on thoughts such as "everything is wrong," or "the cards are stacked against me." Think how great your life will be when good things start flowing into your life. If present conditions aren't to your liking, they will straighten out eventually. Everything will come out right in the end. That's not just positive thinking—that is reality.

Negative people are always inferring that positive thinking is not reality. What is reality? According to Webster's Dictionary, reality is "the quality or state of being real; the totality of real things and events; a preoccupation with facts." Let's look at the facts. Our thoughts produce our feelings (a fact). Positive thoughts produce positive feelings (a fact). Negative thoughts produce negative feelings (a fact). These are facts concerning reality. Now let me ask you. Since you have a choice as to what you think—you do know you can choose your thoughts—do you want positive feelings or negative feelings? Positive feelings produce happiness, negative feelings produce depression. Which reality do you prefer?

Our thoughts are manifested by the immutable Law of Cause and Effect. No man or woman can be happy who lives in a continual state of negativity. This is why the Bible says, "As a man thinketh, so is he" (Proverbs 23:7, King James Version).

In the next chapter, we'll examine how you can change your thinking and change whatever you want to change in your life.

CHAPTER 8

Change Your Thinking and Change Your Life

When I ask people if they could change anything about their life what they would change, most people say they would change their financial situation. Most feel that more money would solve some of their problems. Many fear poverty. They are working hard day after day and just getting by.

Have you ever wondered what attracts wealth to some and poverty to others? If you desire to change your financial picture from poverty to abundance and prosperity, you will, no doubt, welcome what I'm about to share with you because I'm going to show you how to change poverty-thinking to prosperity-thinking. I'll show you how to attract the things you desire including the financial resources you desperately need. By changing your thinking in this area or any other area of your life, you can create for yourself a magnificent future.

Let's look at the facts. The world we live in programs our mind toward poverty. Often we are told it is immoral for some to be prosperous and for others to live in poverty. Often we hear that there is only so much to go around. Resources are limited so we must all share.

The truth is resources are only limited if we think they are. As a matter of fact, the Creator has created more than enough for everyone and is still creating right down to the present moment. Creating is what the Creator does. The Creator doesn't stop creating, doesn't even rest or sleep. The Creator simply creates.

Let's do some critical thinking. Do you think for one minute the Creator of all life would create some of his children to live in poverty and some to live in prosperity? Let me ask you, what kind of parent would choose one child over another? What kind of parent would choose to give one child the gifts of wealth, health, and happiness and choose poverty for another child? No good parent could do this. Neither could the Divine Parent. There is enough for everyone! The universe we live in has unlimited resources, and the Creator continues to create more. In fact, it's even better than it first appears. The Creator has made it possible for us to be co-Creators in a never-ending creative process. The truth is the Creator has created us so we can think things into existence. We were created in a way that our inner thought actually creates our outer world. If you understand what I've just said, you understand the greatest secret of all times—the Law of Attraction. We attract things into our lives by way of our thoughts. We can change our lives by changing our thoughts.

What I'm suggesting is that an Infinite Creator provides for us through our thoughts. The Creator has provided a way for us to create all we desire, enabling us to be responsible for our own lives. We can literally have all we desire. The Creator treats all of His children equally. It couldn't be any other way. All the Creator's children are equal in the mind of the Creator. Good parents don't love one of their children more than another. They don't shower prosperity on one child and poverty on another.

Now having all we desire is difficult for us. We have been taught from a child up we must sacrifice, do without so others can have what they need. The world has adopted the concept of "Live simply so that others may simply live" assuming the Creator has only created a limited amount to go around. Most people don't realize the Divine Creator knows nothing of the concept of shortages. You were not created to live in poverty. In fact, it is sacrilegious to believe that an all-loving Creator would create a world where resources are in short supply. Isn't it amazing that any thinking person could look at a world of plenty and see shortages?

I invite you to look around and awaken yourself to a world of abundance. Imagine everyone living in abundance. Start seeking and thinking abundance and change your situation from poverty to abundance. When the Creator supplies you with more than you need, you'll want to share with others. The Creator has provided plenty for all His children hoping each will claim what they need. Look at it this way. The Creator is offering you all these resources as a gift. You have only to receive the gift. Let go of all past thoughts of poverty. Learn to live forward with faith in the Creator's universal laws. Keep reading as I teach you how to apply the Law of Abundance to your daily living and watch what happens.

Start thinking this moment of abundance. Trust the Creator. Clear your consciousness daily of all thoughts of poverty and learn to manifest abundance. Abundance is everywhere. In fact, the major religions and great teachers of the world have told people of an abundant life. The ideas of progress, improvement, and human development are major tenets of all great civilizations. Deeply engrained in our psyches, we find hope for the oppressed and hope for those living in poverty. This hope comes through our oneness with the Divine Creator who has created everything. The Creator is not limited. We are not limited. Creation is not limited.

As the Christ of Judea claimed oneness with the Creator, he felt no limitations. Even death could not stop him. He knew the Creator would make all things work together for good. It couldn't be any other way since the Creator was only good. He taught there was only one Divine Creator, and he trusted the Creator to provide whatever he needed. He told his disciples that the Creator would do for them whatever they asked when they asked believing. He taught them that whatever they believed they would receive, which—by the way—is a restatement of a universal law: **BE IT DONE UNTO YOU AS YOU BELIEVE.** If we believe, we can do big things. In fact, we'll manifest big things. Unfortunately, if all we believe we can do are small things, we will manifest small things. In other words, we create in our minds the mutual equivalent of what we receive.

Let's apply what I've just said to a business. Do people who think small succeed in business? Probably not. Does anyone who thinks they will fail succeed in business? Probably not! A business person must think success to succeed.

Now what about poverty? How can this universal law help to eradicate poverty? Let's go back to the beginning of creation. The Creator did not create poverty. Is that a fair statement? If the Creator didn't create poverty, wouldn't you agree it has to be manmade?

So let's go back in time. Long, long ago and far, far away (that's about as far back as we can go) the world was created. At that time, there was no poverty. There was only abundance. Everyone enjoyed abundance. Every day there was plenty of everything for everyone. Then one day it happened. As more and more people came on the scene, one person started thinking, "I'd better hoard some of this abundance to make sure I have enough for tomorrow." He was unaware of the fact that every day the Creator is creating and the abundance will never be in short supply. The more he hoarded, the more he became paranoid, thinking someday the resources would run out. However, he could never store enough to feel secure. All he could think of was lack. He was always wanting. He began to think of himself as very poor, even destitute. It wasn't long before poverty had taken over his mind. His thoughts were constantly of poverty and poverty was his fate. Poverty originates in the mind. To escape poverty, one has to change one's thinking from lack to abundance.

The Creator created abundance. We were created to live in abundance. We were created to prosper. It is normal for us to desire more for ourselves and for others. It is abnormal to live in poverty. It is abnormal to believe that our living in poverty will help others not live in poverty. In fact, we're not helping ourselves or anyone else if we become destitute because others will have to take care of us. Needless to say, we will have nothing to share.

Start today to think of abundance. It's true that thoughts do become things. Here's how it works. Whatever you deposit in your subconscious mind is manifested in your outer life. Think abundance. Normal people desire to be blessed, prosperous, and enriched in all ways. They inspire others and have no desire to be dependent upon anyone.

Every morning take ten minutes to meditate upon the abundance that the Creator has placed within your reach. Whatever you sow in your subconscious mind, you shall reap. Therefore, sow abundance.

You can actually see abundance in all things. Look around you at nature. Nature is constantly growing and expanding. Nature cannot help but follow the Law of Infinite Increase. What applies in nature also applies on the human plane. The only difference is we have a choice as to whether or not we utilize the Law of Infinite Increase.

To start the journey to prosperity, start applying the Law of Infinite Increase. Believe that a Divine Creator provides abundance for everyone. You will discover that abundance is not an outer possession but an inner realization. It starts with you being appreciative of what you have, knowing that the Divine Creator will enable you to manifest more and more in your life as your thinking changes from lack to abundance. Every day you have the opportunity to manifest abundance. You have the opportunity to advance and grow. As you continue to imagine abundance:

1. Never be envious of others and what they have.
2. Always wish others well. Recognizing their success only adds to your success.
3. Cast out of your mind all deceit.
4. Do not engage in any form of trickery, jealousy, or chicanery. It will come back on you.
5. Never fear lack. Believe and trust in abundance.
6. Do not hoard. There will always be plenty for tomorrow.

A few days ago, I read a true story of hoarding. Years ago during the 1930s, coffee was in short supply. A woman in Chicago, Illinois stocked in her cupboard all the coffee she could buy. She borrowed coffee from friends and neighbors for her personal use to keep from using her own supply. One Sunday, while she was at church, thieves broke into her home. They were delighted to find her stash of coffee and quickly loaded it into their truck along with many of her other possessions. However, before the thieves robbed her, she had already robbed herself mentally by hoarding the supply of coffee. Each day as she thought of her stash of coffee, her subconscious mind was thinking shortage. It is not a coincidence that in the end she experienced the shortage she had imagined.

Do not allow your mind to get caught up in thinking of lack. Thinking of lack produces feelings of lack, which will condition your mind to consistently think of lack and eventually you will experience lack.

Whatever you sow in your mind you shall reap. This is the principle of sowing and reaping. Whatever thoughts you have in your mind you will manifest in your outer life. If you think that some people are just lucky to manifest good things, think again. Listen—I'm Irish and I'm telling you the truth. There is no such thing as luck. The events and circumstances that occur in your life are a direct result of your thoughts.

Here is how to get what you desire. First, decide specifically what you desire. Use the conscious part of your mind and the subconscious part to the maximum. Let's go over once again how this works. As stated previously, whatever is held repeatedly in consciousness will eventually seep into your subconscious. Your subconscious mind will start to work to manifest your desires. Your subconscious has within it the power to complete and perfect your every sincere desire. Here's an exercise that will help you to get started.

- Make a list of your desires. Be specific.
- Read your desires at least three times each day; preferably morning, noon, and night.
- Think about your list of desires as often as possible during the day. It is your thoughts that start the manifestation process.
- Don't talk to anyone else about your desires. Many people will be more than happy to tell you you're dreaming. They don't believe your desires will be manifested.
- Memorize your list of desires and imagine yourself achieving each desire. As things start to happen, be grateful for each manifestation.
- Help others to learn how they, too, can manifest their desires.

You may be thinking: Does this really work? Does my thinking produce things in my outer life? The answer is yes. This is the real world of reality.

In the next chapter, we'll discuss reality.

CHAPTER 9

The World of Reality

A few decades ago when people talked of something impossible, someone would comment, "Well that's about as crazy as trying to put a man on the moon," suggesting that putting a man on the moon was impossible. It's funny how impossible things become possible in a few short years.

Have you ever heard the old saying, "He didn't know that it couldn't be done so he did it"? It's amazing how many things we can do when we stop placing limitations on ourselves.

When you were young, you were fearless and full of confidence. You thought you could do anything. Unfortunately, as life progressed, you became a little less confident. You were told that everyone has limitations. Many things you wanted to do seemed impossible. You felt they just couldn't be done. You bought into the current limited thought and your world became smaller.

Discard your list of things that can't be done and I'll show you how to break free from a very limited sense of reality. Let's get rid of your list of "can't be dones" and break free from the mental prison in which you find yourself. Let me warn you—your sense of reality will change. I'll show you a way to accomplish your greatest desires. I'll help you discover all the good things that are right in front of you.

Most of us limit our reality by thinking thoughts that limit our existence—thoughts such as: this can't be done, I could never do that, and no one could do that. Have you noticed your reality gets smaller as you engage in limited thinking? Change your thinking!

First, recognize that your reality is determined by your thoughts. It's to your advantage to focus on thoughts of things you desire, leaving nothing to luck or chance. Now it is mandatory that you do your own thinking if you want to create a larger reality for yourself. Avoid getting caught in the thought current of society. The thought current is usually something other than what you desire. By doing your own thinking, you can stop picking up other people's baggage. You have enough baggage of your own.

It would be wonderful if thought currents were visible, then you could see how they flow to and from people. This is really important because whatever current of thought you find yourself in, you will be attracted to others with a similar thought current. If you are in low spirits, you will find yourself being pulled toward others with low spirits. If you are in high spirits, you'll find yourself being attracted to others in high spirits. Beware—if you are attracted to low spirits or despondent spirits for any length of time, your mind will become despondent. Likewise, if you are attracted to high-spirited people, you'll share in their joy.

Unfortunately, the same applies to thought currents of evil, crime, or immorality. Persons associating with these currents become, for a time, one with such current. If you desire to go in the opposite direction, associate yourself with currents of good, love, beauty, and life because association with such currents will pay huge dividends.

Choose carefully the groups you frequent. If a group of people talk of any form of disease or suffering, of death and dying agonies, they are cultivating an unhealthy current that will lead to disaster. If you talk about sickness, you invite a current of sickly thoughts into your mind, and its ill result will, in time, materialize itself in your physical body.

Here is an example. I was sitting in church only a few weeks ago waiting for the service to begin. In the pew behind me, I overheard a group of people talking about their illnesses. They were reveling in each other's agony. The reader may think I'm not empathetic, but I couldn't help but feel their intense satisfaction in sharing their illnesses. They did not have a clue what their conversation was doing to them. We humans are inclined to share our illnesses with anyone who has a sympathetic ear. However, the more we talk about illnesses, the worse it gets. We are imagining illness instead of health. We have far more to do in the process of healing ourselves than we realize. Our focus must be on getting well, becoming healthy, and seeing ourselves whole.

This way we draw to ourselves a thought current of health and wellness. As we ponder daily these qualities, we make them a part of ourselves. Our desire is to be vigorous, robust, hearty, able-bodied, and in sound condition. All of us must endeavor to get ourselves into the thought currents of things that are beneficial. Avoid thoughts of illness and suffering at all costs. Keep healthy thoughts as you are evolving into a strong, healthy, robust individual. Focus on thoughts of things you desire.

Realize that you are bombarded daily by the news with thoughts of horrors. You will be informed of every murder, theft, or crime which the media chronicles every twenty-four hours. Do not—I repeat—do not internalize this stuff. Pay attention to what you are inviting into your mind. Choose carefully the books you read, the news you watch, and the company you keep. Beware of internalizing thought currents of fear and failure. The streets are full of people who, if fearing nothing else, fear they are going to be late for their next appointment.

As you create your new reality, remember; whatever thought is most held in your mind is most materialized in your living. Now let's look at some helpful hints to assist you in creating a new reality.

1. Refuse to accept any disagreeable thought current that would jeopardize your positive mental condition. Train your mind to shut out negative thoughts that could harm you. Bar tightly the door to weakness and keep open only the door to strength.
2. Rely on your inner strength to bring you out of any struggles. The Infinite Spirit working through your subconscious mind will bring many ideas to assist you. For instance, it may suggest medicines, foods, surroundings, and changes that will not only help you temporarily, but permanently. A cheerful, hopeful disposition will assist you in getting out of any harmful, societal thought current.
3. Trust your inner power and watch how quickly your reality is renewed.

When you are in the thought current of the Creative Spirit that functions through your mind, there is absolutely nothing to fear. Good things will come to you with very little physical or external effort. You can forget about toiling and striving, working yourself literally to death to accomplish things. A reality filled with abundance will come to you greater than you ever imagined. You will find that the more you get in touch with the Creative Spirit, exhausting toil is not required. When you commit yourself to the thought current of the Creative Spirit, all things needful will come your way.

As you experience your new reality, you may, for a time, experience uneasiness. This is because the new things happening to you make you more sensitive. As the new is driving out the old, it is like house cleaning. The process usually involves a great deal of dust and disturbance. You are cleaning your mind to accommodate the Creative Spirit of the universe. You are in the process of creating for yourself a new reality. In the future, there will be no limit to the things you can do. You will accomplish miracles. Some will say you have an inner power that is comparable to magic.

You will realize the Creative Spirit of the universe has created a new reality for you by renewing or remaking your mind. You will become one with the Creative Spirit of the universe. Let's go over the process you must use to create your new reality. First, the mind must be at rest. The mind at rest will draw spiritual elements and nourishment from the Creative Spirit, a spirit so healthy that it cannot know or feel any evil thought current and it knows how to avoid all negative thought currents.

You must be at rest to invite the Creative Spirit into your life. This doesn't come easy. A cluttered mind is a mind without rest. You must set aside time each day to meditate, to turn your mind from the channels in which it has been rushing and running to a more relaxed state. Such meditative moments of thought give the mind and body the rest needed to function properly. As your mind starts to function properly, you will be empowered to do things you never thought possible. You will be on your way to creating a new reality; a reality of growth, a reality where you can create your every desire. You are about to enter a whole new level of learning. An inner impulse to learn more, to become more, and to advance will begin to surface in your thoughts. Ernest Holmes referred to this inner impulse as the Divine urge.[15] The Divine urge will begin to permeate your every living moment as it whispers in your ear "grow, advance, flourish...." You have to be more tomorrow than you are today.

The universal Law of Growth will become a part of your daily experience. The Law of Growth implies if you are not growing, you are stagnating. It is imperative that every living thing must grow or it dies.

There is no middle ground. There is no standing still. Physically, mentally, and spiritually we are either growing or dying.

As we trust the Creative Spirit, we can live a reality without limitations. We are forever learning, forever growing, and knowing there will always be more. Our job is to align ourselves with the Creative Spirit and patiently stay the course as we continue to grow. We live in a universe that holds unlimited possibilities for us and is guiding us toward our maximum potential, toward a life without limits.

Now that you have created for yourself a new reality with unlimited possibilities through the power of the Creative Spirit of the Universe, in Part Two we'll show you how you can use the knowledge you have gained to achieve prosperity.

PART TWO

CHAPTER 10

Achieving Prosperity

Many people grew up being told that prosperity is something only a few people manage to achieve. I'll bet most of you were told prosperity is the result of years of hard work and careful savings. That "work and save" nonsense was hammered into your minds. Most of you were never told you were capable of achieving prosperity. In fact, you were told just the opposite. Some were told that they would "never amount to a hill of beans." If you talked of achieving great things, you were told you were dreaming. You may have been told you were having delusions of grandeur. Some folks went so far as to say, "Nobody we know has ever amounted to anything." Do you remember anyone saying, "Look at me. I wasn't born prosperous, but I *became* prosperous"? Did you hear anything like that? Most of you were never encouraged to become prosperous. You were discouraged as you were told prosperity results from years of hard work and diligent saving. If you looked around, you saw many who worked a twelve-hour day, five to six days a week for most of their lives, and they ended up barely surviving on social security. Some of you concluded that the journey to prosperity involves more than hard work and careful savings. Historically, all kinds of myths have circulated about prosperity. Let's look at some of these myths.

MYTHS ABOUT PROSPERITY

- Prosperity results from years of hard work and diligent savings.
- You have to have an education to be prosperous.
- Some people are too young to be prosperous. They haven't lived long enough.
- Some people are too old to be prosperous. They've waited too long.
- You have to have certain skills to be prosperous.
- Some folks are just lucky enough to be prosperous.
- Women shouldn't be more prosperous than their husbands.
- People who are prosperous worship the almighty dollar.
- Women don't need to be prosperous if they have husbands who will take care of them.
- You can't be prosperous and be happy.
- You can't be spiritual and be prosperous.
- All prosperous people are greedy.
- Some people don't deserve to be prosperous.
- If you're prosperous, you cause others to suffer poverty.
- God doesn't like prosperous people.

The list goes on and on, but not a single one of these myths is true. I'm going to ask you to empty your mind of them. All of these myths go in File 13 (trash can). In Part Two, you are going to let go of the myths and replace them with truths that will lead to prosperity. My definition of prosperity is taken from Emmet Fox who says, "Prosperity means freedom from nagging fears concerning the necessaries of life."[16] If you stopped working today, how many days would you survive? Would you be able to trust yourself to secure your future? One of the greatest accomplishments any of us can make in life is to secure our future. To do so, you must learn to walk the way of Truth. The greatest teacher can do no more than walk the way of Truth and point it out to you. You must walk it for yourself. Now let's address some of the truths about prosperity.

PROSPERITY TRUTHS

- Prosperity is not a thing of favor or chance but is the result of consistent thinking in a certain way. It is the effect of a desire held in thought over a period of time.
- The journey to prosperity is paved with strong, positive thoughts.
- Your prosperity journey begins by recognizing what you already have.
- You were created to be prosperous.
- Prosperous people learn to set goals and live by them.
- Prosperous people have more than they need so they can share with others.
- Your prosperity will bring joy to you and to others.
- Your subconscious mind will direct you on your prosperity journey.
- Positive affirmations attract prosperity.
- Prosperous people love what they do.
- Prosperous people have faith in their own abilities and accomplish far more than those who have no confidence in themselves.
- The more you help others to be prosperous, the more prosperous you will be.
- Prosperity is to be enjoyed.
- Prosperous people balance their giving to others with careful, pleasurable spending.
- Prosperous people learn not to economize all the time because economizing can create a poverty consciousness.
- Prosperous people know it's okay to like money as long as you don't fall in love with it.
- Prosperous people know that people who say they have no interest in prosperity end up in poverty.
- Prosperous people know what you think in your mind and feel deep down in your heart will be what you experience in life.
- Prosperous people feel good about themselves and bring joy into the lives of others.

- People who are prosperous keep working long after they have made more money than they can spend.

In Part Two of this book you will learn:

- To recognize and appreciate what you already have
- How to communicate to your subconscious mind and allow it to direct you on your prosperity journey
- How to use positive affirmations to attract prosperity
- To look for new opportunities to bring additional prosperity into your life
- To have confidence in your own abilities
- The importance of helping others to be prosperous
- Prosperity is to be enjoyed.
- How to balance your giving to others with giving to yourself in responsible spending and to reward yourself periodically
- Refrain from economizing all the time because it can create a poverty consciousness.
- How to have a healthy "like" for money and not become obsessed with it
- It's okay to desire prosperity.
- How to change your thoughts so you can experience life as you want it to be
- To feel good about yourself and your ability to bring joy to the lives of others
- How to tap into the Infinite Intelligence of the Universe

Prosperity is not a thing of favor or chance, but is the result of consistent thinking in a certain way. It is the effect of a desire held in thought over a period of time.

Let's look at the facts. Achieving financial prosperity is certainly not a result of environment. We see rich people and poor people living side by side. Getting rich is not due to talent. We see many talented people who remain poor. Others who have very little talent become rich. Achieving financial prosperity is not a result of vocation. When you study people in the same vocation, one is rich and another is poor.

The first great discovery made by man was that he could think. By changing his thoughts, he could remold his affairs, and by right thinking he could bring new conditions into his life, especially prosperity. The truth is you can achieve prosperity in any environment, with any amount of talent, and in any vocation with a minimum of intelligence if you are willing to think prosperity and do things in a certain way. If like causes always produce like effects, then any man or woman who does things in a certain way can become prosperous. Your thoughts objectify themselves. In simple terms, you become what you think about all day. This is the Law of Mind. You can create in your mind an accurate mental picture of what you desire, and it will eventually appear in your outer world.

Never devalue your own capacities, skills, or potential. Have faith in yourself and clear your mind of fear and doubt. You are standing on the threshold of a new era. The time has arrived when you have the possibility of learning and applying the secret of bringing prosperity into your life. There is an unavoidable tendency to become literally the embodiment of that quality upon which one most thinks. The best thing you can do is focus on the right thoughts followed by right effort. There is within each of us a desire to know more and to be more.

As you apply what you have learned in this book, you'll discover that your power to think is infinite. Your power to create with your thoughts is unlimited. Your ability to think and understand in a prosperous way can get you anything you desire. You can even change the biochemistry of your brain. You no longer have to be programmed for failure or defeat.

Throughout history, great teachers and philosophers have discovered an incredible secret: Your thoughts create your destiny. Thinking in a certain way can lead to prosperity. Your prosperity depends on the grandeur of your thoughts.

As Marcus Aurelius, a great Roman emperor, said, "A man's life is what his thoughts make it."[17] Ralph Waldo Emerson wrote, "A man is what he thinks about all day long."[18] George Bernard Shaw wrote, "You imagine what you desire. You will want what you imagine. You make what you will."[19]

For centuries, great religious teachers have taught this concept. The Christ of Judea said, "…all things can be done for the one who believes" (Mark 9:23, NRSV). Every belief you have is the sum total of several thoughts. What you believe you shall receive.

Gautama Buddha wrote, "All that we are is the result of what we have thought."[20] Our minds are the last frontier on Planet Earth. The more we learn how to use the mind, the more unlimited our possibilities will be. You must rely on your inner power and your inner voice. While it is true you are partially a product of your ancestors' thoughts and conditions, you are mostly a product of your own past thoughts and present conditions, and your future will be determined by your present thoughts.

Prosperity is the effect of desire held in thought over an extended period of time. You are a beneficiary of life. You did not put the "chicken in the egg" or "the oak tree in the acorn." You did not create your own life, but you can be in the business of receiving more life and creating additional life with your thoughts. You are what your thoughts make you. Therefore, if you think in negative terms, you will achieve negative results. If you think in positive terms, you will achieve positive results. This, my friend, is a simple fact which is the foundation of the astonishing Law of Prosperity. Your outer circumstances will mirror your inner thoughts. Therefore, you may want to do some Prosperity Thinking. If poverty has gotten under your skin and inside your brain, you can change your circumstances by Prosperity Thinking. Since your outer circumstances mirror your inner thoughts, it would be to your advantage to do some Prosperity Thinking.

Your mind is like a garden. Whatever you plant in it will grow. You can intentionally cultivate it or allow it to run wild. If you keep your mind free of the weeds of impure thoughts, worry, or fear and plant prosperous thoughts; you will produce the flowers and fruits that grow from prosperous thoughts—fruits such as gratitude, enthusiasm, joy, peace, and other wonderful fruits that lead to a prosperous life. Whatever you plant and cultivate is what you will get in return. If you allow your mind to run wild, it is anybody's guess what you'll get. I can guarantee you will not like what you get because it won't be prosperity. The journey to prosperity is paved with strong, prosperous thoughts held in your mind over an extended period of time. You must pursue your purpose with a fearless heart believing that the future will be a future of prosperity.

CHAPTER 11

The Human Mind Has No Boundaries

I want to let you in on a little secret. The human mind has no boundaries, and there are no limits to what it can do. It will do anything you ask of it. It comes as standard equipment at birth. Everyone gets one free. Because it's free, many people take it for granted and place little value on it. Some people rarely use it and end up in dire circumstances. They are stressed out going from paycheck to paycheck. They are stuck in a cycle they can't get out of. They must have, have, have so they go, go, go and do, do, do! The entire universe is trying to tell them something. Inside their minds, they often hear a voice saying, "There must be a way out of my misery." There is! If you change your thinking and begin to control your thoughts, marvelous things will begin to happen.

With the proper use of your mind, everything you desire in life is achievable, including prosperity. As a matter of fact, everything you need to achieve prosperity you already have: your mind, your soul, your physical body, your hopes, dreams, ambitions, intelligence, and the love of family and friends. You may be thinking right now that you don't have any of these things, but you do. You already have these priceless possessions. Your journey to prosperity starts as you recognize what you already have. The journey of a thousand miles begins with this important step.

Your first step is **BE GRATEFUL AND RECOGNIZE WHAT YOU ALREADY HAVE.** You already have the gift of life. All you need do is recognize it, accept it, and be grateful. Gratitude will shift your focus from things you don't have to things you do have. Once you start recognizing what you have, your whole life will change for the better. In fact, nothing can possibly remain the same because you are focusing on the things you have instead of the things you don't have. Gratitude is the mature emotion. Grateful people have a deep appreciation of benefits received. They look for and expect good things to come their way. They look for the good in themselves and others and they find it. They realize that no one starts at the top. They are happy right where they are.

Carl Sandburg has a wonderful story of a Kansas Sodbuster.

> *The sodbuster leaned on the gate post one day thinking about what corn he might plant next year, trying to calculate why God made the grasshopper, why two days of hot winds smothered the life out of a stand of wheat, why there was so much difference in the price he got for his grain and the price he heard quoted on the news. Suddenly, a stranger drove up in a covered wagon. "What kind of folks live around here?" the stranger asked.*
>
> *"Well, stranger, what kind of folks live in the country you came from?"*
>
> *Well," said the stranger, "mostly low down, lying, thieving, gossiping, backbiting people."*
>
> *After a few seconds, the sodbuster replied, "Well, I guess that's the kind of folks you'll find here."*
>
> *The stranger blended into the dusty trees as he drove on.*
>
> *Another newcomer drove up. "What kind of folks live around here?" the stranger asked.*
>
> *Again the sodbuster replied, "Well, stranger, what kind of folks was there in the country you came from?"*
>
> *The friendly stranger smiled, "Well, those was mostly decent, hardworking, law-abiding, friendly lot of people."*
>
> *Again the sodbuster said, "Well, I guess that's about the kind of folks you'll find around here."*
>
> *And the second wagon moved on.*[21]

The world cooperates with us conforming to our thoughts and expectations. If you are looking for prosperity, start by recognizing how prosperous you already are. Your attitude is determined by your thoughts! Your thoughts, in turn, determine your feelings. Your world will mirror your thoughts and feelings. Whatever is going on inside your mind will eventually appear in your outside world. Your external world will exactly correspond to your inner world.

Your thoughts literally determine your life. They help you to achieve what you desire or they keep you from achieving what you desire. Your thoughts will enhance or narrow the scope of your life. Your world will either get larger or smaller, depending on your thoughts. If your thoughts are of prosperity, your world will grow larger. If your thoughts are of lack or scarcity, your world will become smaller. To learn how to think is to learn how to live. You will inevitably attract people, events, and circumstances into your life that harmonize with your dominant thought.

None of us have to be imprisoned by fixed attitudes and expectations. Using your mind can pay huge dividends. In John Milton's *Paradise Lost* Satan says, "The mind is its own place and in itself can make a heaven of hell and a hell of heaven."[22] You are free to choose the contents of your conscious mind. Countless millions are living in a virtual heaven of opportunity. Prosperity is everywhere, yet they turn life into a living hell. They have every opportunity to choose an attitude of love, yet they hate; every opportunity to trust, yet they mistrust; every opportunity to live a prosperous life, yet they live in poverty often condemning prosperity. They don't realize you lose what you condemn. Their attitude is often one of "nothing good ever happens to me." They could share in the prosperity of the world, yet they sit and grumble feeling life and prosperity have passed them by. They have not discovered that you create your own misery or your own happiness. There seems to be something in the human thought that says man is poor, man is limited, there is lack of opportunity, and times are hard. Nobody wants what "I" have to offer. No person achieves prosperity who thinks this way. You must reverse your thinking if you find yourself going in this direction. Your mind needs to be focused on Prosperity Thinking.

The Roman philosopher Seneca put it this way: "A great, a good, and a right mind is a kind of divinity lodged in flesh and may be the blessing of a slave as well as a prince."[23] Whatever you think about and concentrate upon repeatedly will become a part of your inner and outer life.

Chaucer wrote, "My mind to me a kingdom is. Such present joy therein I find that it excels all other bliss that earth affords."[24] Your mind is your kingdom, and you are the reigning monarch. You decide what your kingdom will be—bleak or bountiful, prosperous or poor, interesting or dull, happy or unhappy. Your attitudes, your expectations, and your thoughts are up to you. Could it be any easier? You can fashion your own future. True prosperity is always granted to the heart that abounds with integrity, trust, generosity, love, and Prosperity Thinking.

CHAPTER 12

You Were Born to be Prosperous!

Many people assume that it is the will of a Higher Power that they were born in poverty when just the opposite is true. If most parents want prosperity for all their children, isn't it reasonable that God wants the same thing for all God's children? The Will of a Divine Creator for all life can only be something glorious, beautiful, and prosperous since poverty demoralizes. You were created to prosper. In fact, each person is created with an inner power to assist them with prosperity. However, approximately 95% of the world's population never discover this inner power. We listen to people who tell us not to expect too much out of life and we won't be disappointed, people who tell us the best we can expect is to go to work every day, pay our bills, and raise our children to do the same. Some of you have seen the bumper sticker, "I owe, I owe, so off to work I go." Too often, life is viewed as depressing or devastating. There is the feeling that we must accept what is. The new expression of our 21st century is "It is what it is."

It's no wonder the suicide rate continues to increase. Everywhere dreams are shattered. Some people have learned to enjoy spreading "gloom and doom." They feel if they have to suffer, everyone else should suffer along with them. Misery loves company. These people are unaware of what they are doing. Have you ever tried to tell someone your dreams? Some people will tell you all the reasons why you can't accomplish your dreams. They are more than happy to help you fail. They feel they don't deserve to be prosperous and neither do you. Your prosperity will only remind them of their failure. This is why it is essential for you to "direct" your life story and "star" in it. When you tell others of your dreams, some will confront you with reverse autosuggestion. They will tell you all the reasons why you can't accomplish your dreams. They will tell you that you can't possibly succeed.

I once overheard a sixteen-year-old musical performer tell a person he was going to perform before large audiences someday. The person responded, "Son, you are dreaming. Hardly anyone succeeds in music these days." Hearing what this young man was told, I pulled him aside and said, "Don't believe what you were just told. Follow your dream. Don't allow anyone to stand in your way. You will succeed." Feeling good about ourselves is necessary to develop a prosperity consciousness. We must be relaxed, calm, and self-assured as we walk through life. By the way, the young man I just mentioned is now in his thirties. He has performed before great crowds of people. His dream came true. He not only accomplished his teenage dream, he has achieved one big dream after another. He is prosperous because his mind is filled with Prosperity Thinking.

Be careful who you share your dreams with. Find friends who will encourage you to be prosperous. Friends who are negative about your dreams should be "friends at a distance." As you encounter negative people, you must communicate with them. Don't refuse to talk to them, but refuse to accept their false philosophy of life. You have a valuable contribution to make.

Prosperity is available to anyone who desires it. It's available to anyone who has the courage to follow their dream. You can do whatever you want to do. Prosperous people know that the game of prosperity, like the game of golf, is won or lost in your head. The simple desire to do something is proof that you have the power within to do it. As you achieve your dreams, others will stop telling you that you can't be prosperous because inevitably they will see you achieve what they said you couldn't achieve. As you go through life, hold on to your dreams and help others around you hold on to their dreams. Don't oppose or harm anyone. As you go through life, desire to be no one's enemy and everyone's friend. Set goals to move from poverty to prosperity, from poverty to power, from dependency to self-reliance. You must realize that no one is destined to live in a shack, dress in rags, or go hungry. Reject and let go of all the darkness and ignorance of the world and know that you possess the equipment, power and knowledge you need to become prosperous. Realize that prosperity means much more than money. Real prosperity includes health, prestige, social status, healthy relationships, and peace of mind. It means you experience the wonderful feeling of placing your head on your pillow at night knowing you are at peace with the world and all is well in your life.

CHAPTER 13

Prosperous People Learn to Live by the Laws of Achievement

If you are determined to be prosperous, no one will be able to stop you. The more you affirm your goals and realize them as a reality, the more intense will be your desire. If you know where you want to go, you can always find a way to get there.

To be prosperous, you need to belong to one of two groups. The first group consists of people who have discovered some natural interests—what they are best fitted to do. For some, it is a branch of science. For others, it may be one of the arts. An example is a physician who is so wrapped up in medicine that even after a sixteen-hour day, he or she can't wait to get back to it. These people are happiest and most prosperous when they are pursuing their natural interest. Their work is a magnet for them, and they can't imagine doing anything else. They love their work, and this love of work helps them achieve goal after goal. They are doing what they are naturally inclined to do. Everything they do is triggered by their inner desires, urges, and instincts.

The second group is made up of people who are driven by goals. They know what they want and keep pursuing goal after goal until they achieve their dreams. What they truly value and believe is expressed in their actions. They realize one great idea can be worth millions. As soon as one goal is met, they start to work on others. The Law of Increase is mathematically certain for the person who is advancing forward toward an invigorating goal. A person with a goal and a clear purpose can make progress even on the roughest road. They have both short-term and long-term goals. Their short-term goals can be achieved in a short span of time. Their long-term goals may take as long as five years to achieve. Some examples of long-term goals are: a degree in higher education, a certain amount of money invested, buying a home, or starting a business.

Their short-term goals break up the monotony of the long haul. You can have anything you want if you set goals and work to achieve them. Achieving short-term goals encourages you to work on success after success on your journey to prosperity. Every success builds self-confidence. You need lots of self-confidence to stay positive. The reason people fail is lack of self-confidence. Here is how it happens with most people. They fail in some activity early in their life and fear it will happen again. They may have parents or other adults in their life who were never satisfied with their performance leaving them with a feeling of inferiority. A woman I know grew up in a family where A's in school were not good enough. She brought home straight A's on her report card, but her father told her she could do better. If she made 98 percent she should have made 100 percent. To this day, she puts herself down constantly. She criticizes her talents. She can't appreciate the talent she has because she feels she should always do better.

Some people have tasted success only to have it followed by some sort of failure, and have let that setback dominate their thinking and doom them to failure. To break this failure pattern, they must set and achieve goals. This will help them develop self-confidence, which is essential to prosperity. Please listen to what I am about to say—never mind what people think of you. Some will overestimate your possibilities, others will underestimate you, but until you believe in yourself, you will never be prosperous.

If someone says you are a failure, tell yourself you were born to be prosperous. Every time you are told you are going to be defeated, use it as a stimulus to increase your faith in the inner power the Creator has placed within you. No one can control your thinking unless you allow them. You are who you think you are. Learn to set goals and achieve them and you will become more and more prosperous. You must continue to grow as you move forward. Growth is a law of life. You are either growing or moving forward or you are going backward. You cannot stand still for very long.

There is no stopping the person who is advancing forward. For years, the industrial system kept the masses in poverty because they did not know they could advance forward. As soon as the masses discovered they could move forward, nothing could stop them.

If you desire to do big things, set big goals. If you have a small concept of life, you will always do small things. If you want to do big things, get over the old idea you were meant to sell peanuts. Some people are afraid of greatness because they are so tied to littleness. Do not fear superiors or bad personalities. Keep working toward your goals of success avoiding all distractions. When the tide of opportunity flows in a different direction, keep your thoughts on prosperity and go with the flow of the tide of opportunity. To think prosperity in the midst of poverty requires power, but one who acquires this power becomes a mastermind with the ability to conquer fate and have whatever one wants.

CHAPTER 14

Learn How to Communicate with Your Subconscious Mind

Now that you realize you were created to be prosperous, start to visualize yourself as prosperous, happy, and healthy. Whatever you think and desire you will impress on your subconscious mind, and it will be manifested in your outer experience. If you are thinking about things you don't want, change your thinking. When you change your inner concept, your outer circumstances will change. The Law of Mind is indestructible, immutable, and timeless. Like all other laws of the universe, it never fails.

This is the Master Secret of all ages: **YOUR SUBCONSCIOUS MIND HAS THE MARVELOUS POWER TO CREATE WHATEVER IS IMPRESSED UPON IT.** The person who is knowledgeable of the workings of the subconscious mind will never worry about anything, especially economic conditions. I'm going to go into detail on this because it is the very foundation of becoming prosperous. By using the Law of Mind and the hidden power of your subconscious mind, you can bring into your life every good thing you need to become prosperous as you develop a mind that is advancing toward prosperity. By abiding in a consciousness of Prosperity Thinking, one will always be provided for regardless of outer circumstances.

Your subconscious mind can generate your every need. All you need do is learn how to use it. If you understand how the marvelous power of your subconscious works, you can apply it to all aspects of your life. You can realize all your hopes and dreams. Your life can become grander, richer, and more prosperous than you ever dreamed. Your reality depends on how much your consciousness has developed. Of course, you will want to seek the highest level of consciousness. As you seek this higher level, everything beneath it will flow into your life. Below is an illustration of a step pyramid of desire:

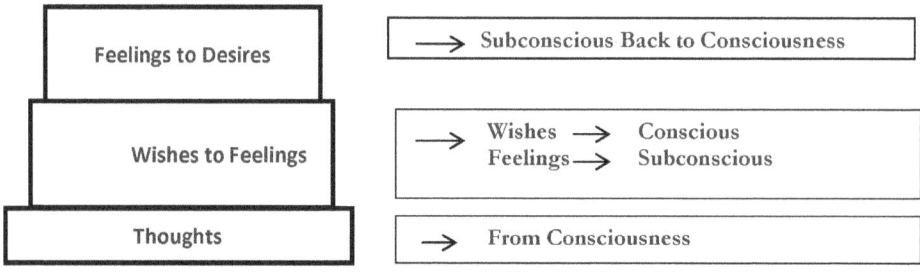

I ask you to keep an open mind and be receptive to what I'm suggesting as we move forward. A mind is like a parachute. It works better when it's open. I will show you how to tap into the Infinite Intelligence of the universe. This Creative Intelligence is behind all new inventions, new discoveries, creative works of art, and all new knowledge. And here is the good news. This awesome Creative Intelligence is available to you through your subconscious mind. You will find solutions to problems that have before baffled you; answers to seemingly impossible questions, and explanations of universal principles that have perplexed humankind for centuries.

This Creative Power can heal troubled minds and broken hearts. It can open doors in your mind that have been locked for decades and liberate you from all kinds of emotional and neurotic bondage. To use this awesome power, you must understand its principles and apply it to whatever you wish to accomplish. Just imagine how your life will change as you apply this incredible power.

As discussed in Part One, your subconscious mind works according to the Law of Belief: **WHAT YOU BELIEVE BECOMES YOUR REALITY.** Whatever you experience in your outer life is produced by your inner thoughts and beliefs. If you change these inner thoughts and beliefs, the outer picture or life experiences will change. Every thought, like a seed sown in the ground falls into your subconscious mind and takes root, thereby producing its own. Good thoughts bear good fruit. Bad thoughts produce bad fruit. Thoughts of lack manifest poverty. Thoughts of abundance manifest prosperity.

The story of your life is really the story of your thoughts and beliefs. If you want to change your story, you must change your thoughts and beliefs. The principle of **"As Within, so Without"** is very critical here. Whatever is on the inside will show up in your outer experiences since your outer experiences are produced by your subconscious mind in reaction to your thoughts and beliefs. To accomplish your desires, you must fill your mind with the things you wish to appear in your life. Now that you know what your subconscious can do, let me tell you how to get it to cooperate with you to help you become prosperous!

As you read in Chapter One, everyone has one mind with which we are gifted at birth. It has two functional parts: the conscious and the subconscious. The conscious function is the most familiar part. It functions like the captain of a ship. Your conscious function directs the ship and sends out orders. Your subconscious follows the orders without question and carries them out. Your conscious mind is the master of your ship. Your subconscious mind works to carry out the orders that come from your conscious mind. Your conscious mind is the reasoning part of your mind. It makes your decisions. While the conscious part of your mind is working, your subconscious is also working. It works automatically, carrying out vital functions such as digestion, circulation, and breathing. While you sleep, your subconscious is busy at work. If you need to go to the bathroom in the middle of the night, it will wake you up. It never stops. It keeps going and going and going. If it stops, you die. Now here is a very important fact you need to know: your subconscious mind has no power of discernment. It will accept any kind of thought; good, bad, or indifferent. It works to carry out whatever thoughts you feed it. As soon as it accepts an idea, it proceeds to go to work on it. It will often use bits and pieces of information that have seeped into it to bring about some condition or event in your life.

Since it does not discern behavior, it does not know whether your thoughts are good for you or bad for you. It starts to work to manifest whatever seeps into it from consciousness. It simply reacts to the impressions given it by your conscious mind. The thoughts you have today will create your tomorrow. The only way you can create for yourself a new tomorrow is to change your thoughts. You are the lord and master of your thoughts. You are the shaper and author of your environment. Your thoughts will imprison or liberate you.

Using your subconscious mind to your advantage is often difficult in a world filled with fear. Fearful thoughts become emotionalized and subjectified and become your reality. Thoughts of fear create feelings of fear. Feelings of fear held over a period of time create fearful emotions. Fearful emotions held in your conscious mind seep into your subconscious mind where the subjective energy of the universe works to create whatever you fear. Here is an example of how this might happen. You fail at something a couple of times and develop a fear of failure. You try out for a part in a play, and you are rejected. You don't get the part, and you start telling yourself: "I'm awful. I'll never get a part. I can't act." You convince yourself that you can't act. You start thinking: "I'd try for a part in another play, but I know I'd only fail." The only way to overcome your fear is to change your thinking. You can counter such thoughts by telling yourself you are good at acting, and keep trying until you get a part. Then you can achieve your dream of being an actor.

You can cause yourself great harm by consciously suggesting to yourself that you are a failure. The power of autosuggestion is strong. It helps you create whatever you desire, but it can also destroy you. Your soul attracts that which you secretly harbor, that which you love, and that which you fear. It reaches the height of its cherished aspirations or falls to the level of its basest fears. It is truly a sad fact that in the midst of plenty, many people live in poverty because of fear. Some fear the economy, some fear they do not have what it takes to succeed, and some fear they have waited too long, afraid they are too old to start. Don't fear being a late starter. Concentrate on being a strong finisher.

Most of us realize we are products of our environment. From the day we are born, we are bombarded with negative suggestions. If we don't know how to counter them, we will unconsciously accept them and bring them into our experience again and again.

Some examples of negative suggestions are:

- You can't
- You'll fail
- You haven't got a chance
- It's no use
- The world is going to the dogs
- You're too old
- You're too young
- Life is an endless grind
- You can't win

The list goes on and on. As a child, many accept these suggestions without question. It's surprising that anyone survives.

The good news is you have the capacity to choose what you believe. The suggestions of others need not control you. You can ignore them by mentally choosing thoughts of life, love, and prosperity. Look at the lives of those who have plenty. You will find that most were thrown into poverty and lack again and again until they conquered poverty in their mind. Most went to work every day amazed, inspired, and motivated because they were passionate about achieving prosperity.

CHAPTER 15

You'll Want to Have More Than You Need So You Can Share with Others

Greedy people become billionaires but they aren't prosperous because they feel wretched, mean, and poor so long as there is another person in their world richer than they are. Truly prosperous people share their resources with others. In his book *On Caring*, Milton Mayeroff writes:

> *Man finds himself by finding his place, and he finds his place by finding appropriate others that need his care and that he needs to care for. Through caring and being cared for, we experience ourselves as a part of nature; we are closest to a person or an idea when we help it grow. Man is at home in his world when he is caring for and being cared for....*[25]

You are to practice the "Golden Rule" whether the other person does or not. No one can sincerely try to help another without helping himself.

As you journey toward prosperity, you will develop a desire to share what you have with others. You will want for others what you want for yourself, and you will find that you enjoy the experience of sharing with others. The desire to be prosperous in every area of your life is perfectly normal. Most people are seeking more of life. Being prosperous may mean obtaining more love, greater peace of mind, owning your dream home, or accomplishing something else you desire. It can mean a sum of money or a bigger income. The person who doesn't desire to have more is abnormal.

As Oscar Wilde said, "There is only one class of people that think more about money than the rich and that is the poor. In fact, the poor can think of nothing else."[26] If the poor only knew they could get what they desire without hurting or competing with any other person and; in fact, actually increase the well-being of others by having the extra resources to do so, they would rejoice in another's good fortune.

Just as bees collect honey without destroying the flowers, wealth can be acquired without harming anyone. Unfortunately, some people believe that the only way to get ahead is at the expense of someone else. From time to time, you'll hear someone say, "Anybody who is prosperous has to be some kind of crook." The person who talks and thinks this way usually suffers from some kind of financial difficulty. They may be bitter over someone else's prosperity. They are not aware that condemning others will cause prosperity to flee from them. When we condemn the prosperity of others, we communicate to our subconscious that prosperity is undesirable. Then our subconscious works to keep us from being prosperous. Rejoice in the prosperity of others knowing your rejoicing will open the door for your own prosperity.

A major reason why some people never achieve prosperity is they feel resources are limited. They think their being prosperous means other persons have to do without. These folks think they are cheating someone else out of something. They don't realize that the only way you can share with others is to have something to share. If you are just barely getting by, you have nothing left to share. You can render to others no greater service than to make the most of yourself. You should never forget that you have something to share with others, and they have something to share with you. The more you have, the more you have to share. Every sane person wants enough money to go around and some extra to share with others.

One of the noblest reasons for desiring prosperity is to have more than you need so you can share with others. The other evening I (Jan) was playing computer Monopoly with our grandson Seth who is nine years old. He was winning the game with over $117,000,000 in cash and millions of dollars in properties. At one point, he said, "I wish this was for real and I had all this money. I would give some to my mom, some to my dad, some to my sister, some to you and PaPa, some to my other Nana and PaPa. Then I would give some to poor people, and have some left for me." This is a child who has been raised in an environment where the children are taught to be grateful for what they have and that it is important to share with others. This is the attitude all adults need to have. Then money would not be looked upon as a bad thing, rich people would not automatically be thought of as greedy, and we would have plenty for ourselves with plenty to share with others. We would work with integrity, generosity, and love. Being aligned with the greatest of values we can experience the greatest satisfaction.

The Divine Creator created everything in abundance. Look around you. You will see abundance in the universe. You cannot count the grains of sand on a single beach. The earth contains untold riches, and it doesn't require an unusual degree of intelligence to see that the Divine Creator is still creating. As impossible as the concept of constant creation may seem, it is nonetheless true. And the best part is you can become a co-Creator with the Divine Creator. You simply create whatever you desire. To learn how to think is to learn how to create for your thoughts go into a Universal Mind that is infinite in its ability to do, to be, and to create. As you apply the Law of Creativity, you realize whatever your mind can conceive and believe you can achieve. You will discover that imagination rules the world. Imagination is more important than facts. Your ability to generate constructive ideas is, to all intents and purposes, infinite.

Start thinking this moment of things you want to create. Place no limits on your subconscious mind. There are simply no limits to what you can accomplish when you recognize your thoughts produce things. Draw on your inner power. Nature provides us with many good examples. A tree is a perfect example. A tree has roots from which it draws life. The roots are generally underground (invisible). Unless the tree draws on the invisible it will never flourish. You have roots that are invisible and connected to a life source. Everything you are is a result of you drawing on the Infinite. Imagine yourself rooted in Infinite Life.

For too long, the world has accepted poverty, degradation, and misery. It has assumed gigantic proportions. Let's eradicate poverty, degradation, and misery by shifting our thinking toward prosperity, plenty, peace, happiness, and joy. We can create all these wonderful things by thinking them into existence. Our circumstances and the circumstances of the world will change as our thinking changes.

You are dealing with an awesome Infinite subconscious power which knows no limits since it can create any idea impressed upon it. You have the ability to transcend all your previous limitations when you understand that your inner thoughts create things in your outer world. Success in life is determined entirely by the thought of the individual. You can make of yourself whatever you choose. Every thought issued from your mind makes you a stronger or weaker person. Therefore, under all circumstances, you must do what is right and trust the universal laws and the Divine Power that is immanent in the universe. Never let go of integrity, generosity, and love for these coupled with energy will lift you into a truly prosperous state.

Growth and increase are a part of nature. It is inherent in each of us to desire more. This is natural and the way it should be. Everyone should desire prosperity in every area of their lives. It is normal for you to want more of life—more love, more peace of mind, and more of all that is good. Our desire for good things is God-given, and you can have all these things without hurting any other person. In fact, as we've stated, possessing these things will give you added potential to share with others. You will want others to discover what you have discovered. You will desire to help others prosper. You will long for the opportunity to serve others. As you give, you will learn that your rewards in life will always be in direct proportion to your service to others. People who practice Prosperity Thinking have a deep desire to help others. They know prosperity is like the tide. It goes out, but it always comes back to the one that shares. You will attract prosperity.

Unexpected and wonderful things will come into your life. People who have something to share with you will appear at the right time. Everything will start to come together for you as your life takes on new meaning and direction. You will feel an overwhelming sense of gratitude.

You will no longer feel something is missing in your life. You will no longer concentrate on shortages or shortcomings. You will realize there is plenty of everything to go around. You will realize that your fortune is not by chance but by the observation of certain fixed laws. You make your own misery, your own unhappiness, and your own prosperity by the thoughts of your mind. Observe the universal laws of nature and make the course corrections needed in your thoughts. You can try hiding your ignorance, but one evening of wine will reveal it. As you make corrections in your thinking and engage in Prosperity Thinking, your life will never be the same. You will feel incredible. You will have a calm look in your eyes and smiling will come as natural as breathing. You will radiate goodwill like an old-fashioned stove radiates heat on a cold morning. You'll be happy and satisfied and you will feel prosperous. Self-confidence will inspire, fill, and permeate your every action. You will have prosperity to share and enough to spare.

CHAPTER 16

How to Attract Prosperity

People who have achieved prosperity will be quick to tell you that a positive mental attitude goes hand-in-hand with success and happiness in virtually every dimension of life. As you journey to prosperity, negative circumstances cannot stop you. Your chief business is to succeed. I must warn you, however, you will encounter negative people, but don't allow them to influence you with their negative philosophy. You have a secret weapon you can use to deal with such people: a simple word can do so much. It has been in your vocabulary since you were a child. When people ask how you are doing, respond, "Great!" It's like having a fly swatter in hand and getting rid of a fly that lands on your floor. You'll stop negative people in their tracks.

Since it's impossible to be prosperous without dealing with all kinds of negative people, a basic understanding of people is required. People are motivated by the need to experience pleasure and avoid pain. They have a need to talk about their problems, but they aren't interested in hearing about yours. They may appear sympathetic as you talk, but be assured they really don't want to talk about your problems. You will encounter people who listen because your problems are worse than their problems. As they listen, they are thinking, "Well my life could be worse!" If their problems happen to be worse than yours, they will come right out and tell you, "You think *you've* got problems! Wait until you hear mine." It's the old cliché of the first person telling their woes doesn't have a chance.

On your journey to prosperity, you learn problems can be solved. In one line of the movie *Fat Albert*, Fat Albert says to Richie, "I don't *have* problems. I *solve* problems." On the journey to prosperity, you learn to solve your problems. You learn not to talk about your problems unless you are discussing them with someone who will assist you in solving them.

When someone asks how you are doing, they really don't want to hear about your problems. They are not asking for a medical report so don't give them a statement on how badly you feel. Trust me; people really don't want to hear about your woes. Just tell them you're great no matter how bad things are.

On your journey to prosperity, believe good things will come to you. This is a fundamental law of nature. Nature does what we believe it will do. A farmer plants a seed. He believes the seed will grow and it does. So plant good thoughts in your mind each day. You will be pleasantly surprised when good things start coming into your life.

At first, you may feel a little uncomfortable saying things are great when they are not, but the word "great" can change your thinking and, in no time, good things will come to you. Now let's discuss how you can change your thinking. Through the process of changing your thinking, you will reverse some life-long patterns. If you believe life is great, you will start seeing some great things in life.

Most of the world believes "seeing is believing." In actuality, the reverse is true—believing is seeing. This principle was introduced to you in Chapter One. This is an absolute principle. Without believing, we can do nothing. By now, this should mean something to you. The principle has been used by great teachers of every generation. Simply stated, the principle is: **IT IS DONE UNTO YOU AS YOU BELIEVE.** Always it is done unto you as you believe. The principle works without fail. When you understand this principle, you will be able to break ties that bind and reverse some unhealthy life-long patterns of thinking. You will then be free to mentally create the things you desire. Once you adopt the right mental attitude and believe that something good is going to happen, things you desire will start appearing in your outer world.

Let's examine the all-important Law of Belief. It is the law of life. What you believe about your life and your world will be done unto you as you believe. Belief forms in your mind as thoughts seep into your subconscious. The belief is then manifested in your outer experiences of life. We are not talking about belief in some ritual, ceremony, or formula. We are talking about the belief in your mind that creates results. Here is a personal application of this very important Law of Belief.

Being positive for me (Larry) wasn't easy. At an early age, I had to reverse some life-long patterns of thinking. I started to work at fifteen years old in a local grocery store. I wanted to do my best since I was fortunate to be asked by the store owner to work in his store. The business he owned was growing so rapidly he needed additional employees. As months went by, a major supermarket across the street could not compete and went out of business. Each day I watched the store owner treat every customer with dignity and respect; the rich, middle class, and poor came in every day and everyone received preferential treatment. When someone asked the owner how he was doing, he would always reply, "Super," "Fantastic," or "Great." At fifteen years old, those words were too positive for my vocabulary. At first, I thought he sounded a little phony, but I wasn't about to be disrespectful to a man who treated everyone with respect. I learned a great deal from him. When people asked me how I was doing, I said "Great" even when I didn't feel great. Little did I know I was on my way to becoming a positive teenager. I quickly learned that people think of you generally as you think of yourself. While others around me were counting their impossibilities, I was counting my possibilities.

My desire to be a prosperous teenager, to dress in the finest fashion, and buy a nice car was of utmost importance to me. I set goals of having the best clothes to wear to school and a car to drive that would be the envy of every high school boy and would get second looks of every high school girl. As weeks went by, I became a positive teenager, and I started achieving my goals. I was one of the best-dressed guys in high school; my shoes, shirts, and jeans were equal and often better than the richest kids who lived on the north side (the richest part) of town. I drove a 1956 Ford Crown Victoria that I traded for a 1957 Chevrolet, which I traded for a 1963 Chevrolet Impala Super Sport. I paid cash for my clothes and my cars and saved money on the side. The owner of the store told everyone that I was one of the hardest-working and most disciplined students he had ever seen. I learned every aspect of the grocery business. Everything I did was successful. I enjoyed my prosperity. I was positive with every customer who walked through the door. I received a raise in salary every year. Life became truly great. I had chosen to live my life by being positive and by being consistent with the highest values and aspirations I knew.

While in college, I realized just how positive I'd become when a college professor referred to me as an "eternal optimist." Looking back, I can honestly say that in my early days I was just pretending to be positive, but the more positive I became, the more I liked it, and the more I felt like I was doing the right thing not only for myself but also for others. Later, as I became a professional person, I worked up to a six-figure salary by Prosperity Thinking. As I retired from one profession, I chose another profession in which I have dedicated the rest of my life to helping others achieve prosperity.

Hindsight is 20/20. Looking back, I realize I unwittingly transformed myself from a negative teenager to a positive, happy responsible prosperity-thinking adult. I must admit, Prosperity Thinking has enriched my life beyond my wildest expectations. I have learned that the quality of life is always determined by one's thoughts and feelings at any given moment.

Speaking to a group a few days ago, I (Larry) told them, "All my needs in life have been met and most of my wants." Life gets better every day. I never cease to tell others how grateful I am for each day of life. Gratitude is the mature emotion. Sure, I've had hard times, troubles, and problems just like any other person, but through all these circumstances, I've used the Law of Belief to bring good things into my life. It's not what happens to you that determines your destiny; it's how you respond to what happens to you that makes all the difference. A positive response to any difficulty will net you incredible results. In all the problems of life, you have the opportunity to learn how to be prosperous, to believe in life, and to become all you can be. When you take charge of your thinking, you will begin to manifest all your desires.

Let's summarize what we've discussed so far. A positive attitude is not something you are born with. Our mental attitude is the direct result of our conscious and unconscious thoughts, which; in turn, become the direct reason for and cause of that which comes into our lives. Our thoughts make our world and fill it with our experiences. By the activity of our thoughts, things come into our lives. A positive attitude is not something that some people have at birth and others do not. It is something you develop. I'm sure there are some prosperous people who are negative, but I would be willing to bet their prosperity is inherited or a product of winning the lottery, not earned. If they continue to be negative, they will eventually lose their prosperity. Let me ask you—do you know a positive, calm, courageous, determined, self-reliant aspiring person? What is their financial condition? They are prosperous! Do you know a negative, weak, whining, fretful person? What's their condition? More than likely they are destitute. Real prosperity is acquired the old-fashioned way—it is earned. The person who earns prosperity believes in being positive and productive, not in being lucky. I jokingly tell people I never buy a lottery ticket. With my great luck, it wouldn't be fair to others. Being prosperous has nothing to do with being lucky and everything to do with being positive and productive.

CHAPTER 17

Once Prosperity is Yours, Look for New Opportunities for Additional Prosperity

Life is always advancing forward. You cannot stand still. You are either growing or declining. No matter where you live or what you do, you are surrounded by opportunities to grow. All you need do is look for them. You must continually look for opportunities to grow, since you are completely responsible for everything you are and for everything you become and achieve.

One of the greatest stories ever told makes this important point. The story told by Dr. Russell Conwell, founder of Temple University, helped him raise more than six million dollars for his school, which in the 1800s and early 1900s was a very hefty sum. The story, *Acres of Diamonds* is the story of a farmer who lived in Africa at the time diamonds were being discovered there. One day a visitor told him of the millions being made by men who were discovering diamond mines. Feeling he needed to get in on the action, the farmer promptly sold his farm and left to search for diamonds. He wandered all over Africa, found no diamonds and; as the story has it, finally penniless, in poor health, and despondent, he threw himself into the river and drowned. Long before this, the man who had purchased the farm found a large unusual-looking stone in a creek which ran through the farm property. He put it on his mantel. One day a visitor stopped by, looked at the stone and told the new owner this unusual-looking stone was the largest diamond the visitor had ever seen and it was worth millions. To the visitor's surprise, the owner of the farm told him the entire farm was covered with stones just like that one. The original owner of the farm who sold the farm to go look for diamonds was sitting on one of the richest diamond mines in the world. He owned acres of diamonds, but he made the mistake of not examining what he had before he ran off in search of diamonds.[27]

Like this farmer, we are sitting on opportunity after opportunity that can be developed. On your prosperity journey, look for opportunities that you can take advantage of daily. There are so many things we simply do not see in our world because we aren't looking for them. You will discover it is just as easy for a prosperity-thinking person to attract millions as it is for a peanut-thinking person to attract peanuts.

You can show different people the same scene and something incredible happens. For instance, a scene of the outskirts of a city might appear to one person as a depressed run-down neighborhood; to another it will appear as a great site for a new manufacturing plant, and to another it will appear as a marvelous opportunity for real-estate development. The world presents to us what we are looking for. Look for opportunities—they are limitless. As Henry David Thoreau wrote: *"We find only the world we look for."*[28]

As you search for new opportunities, imagine them presenting themselves to you. Expect the best to come your way. Whatever you expect with confidence will have a tendency to appear in your life.

The journey to prosperity is forward-moving. If you are not going forward, you are going backward. Going backward is easy. Here is how it often happens. People seek to gratify their desires by the least amount of exertion. They tell themselves that average is good enough. They wake up one morning and they are forty years old. They look in the mirror and get a sinking feeling. They realize those insurance companies know what they are talking about when they deal in mortality tables. They sense a high disparity between what they have accomplished and what they wanted to accomplish.

They ask, "What happened? Where did all those years go? Why didn't I make the most of all those opportunities that lay before me? What did I do with all that time?" Generally, the answer is they got comfortable and settled for something less than they could have achieved. In actuality, we will always get what we settle for. The only way to change our circumstances is to think differently by making the most of every opportunity. No matter what your age, start today to look for opportunities and start moving forward.

Have you noticed that prosperous people love their work? Over and over we're told to work smarter rather than harder. While this is important information to know, it is not what is most important. The most important thing concerning prosperity is for you to love what you do. The one common characteristic among prosperous people is they love their work. Often prosperous people will tell you they left the mainstream to start their own company. This is when their life began to turn around. They wanted to do what they loved to do.

Have you ever wondered why prosperous people keep on working long after they have made more money than they can ever spend? Why would Sam Walton continue to be involved in running Wal-Mart until his death? Why did Bill Cosby keep doing television shows long after he could have retired with a lifestyle most people only dream of? Why did Elvis Presley keep pushing himself to perform when his health was failing? He had more money than he could ever spend. The answer is simple: Prosperous people love what they do.

If you love what you are doing, work is not a chore. People who love what they do are eager to go to work. Contrast that to what you will find with the vast majority of people in our world. Some people literally hate their job. They do not like what they do so they work just hard enough to not get fired. Others find their job tolerable; work is hard, not fun; boring, but they see no way out; they are just marking time.

Work was never meant to be like this. Work was meant to be fun. It doesn't have to be a 9 a.m. to 5 p.m. time of trials and tribulations. By finding the right vocation, you can become prosperous and enjoy what you do at the same time. You can find work that will keep you happy for the rest of your life. As stories of prosperous people are told over and over again, the common thread running through all these stories is they love what they do. In fact, some see work as a hobby.

When your work becomes your hobby, you don't mind going in early or staying late. The time you spend working doesn't matter because you are enjoying yourself. You are having so much fun you can sell your time clock at your next garage sale.

If you don't like what you do, you can change your circumstances. When the opportunity presents itself, make the change. But be sure it is the right opportunity. You don't have to be in a hurry. There is no lack of opportunity. Keep focused as you continue to contemplate your vision. As you imagine your perfect vocation, it will come in time. When it comes, you'll know your "ship has come in."

Now let's suppose you don't know what you want to do. How can you discover your ideal work? First, you need to know there is no blackboard in the sky on which the Creator has written a vocation for you. Your task is to take the talent you have and match it to your desire. You would not have been given a talent if you were not supposed to use it. Next, find what brings you joy and commit yourself to it. If you don't know what brings you joy, ask the question, "What do I enjoy?" Find your joy and use your talent to achieve it. By doing this, you will unleash an avalanche of possibilities; as the right people, circumstances, events, and opportunities come into your life. As you radiate joy, you will attract your perfect vocation.

As you experience joy, learn to enjoy the present. Do not allow yourself, under any pretense, to live in the past. Train yourself to live one day, one hour, one minute at a time. You'll be surprised how your life will change. You will lose nothing, and you will gain much. You will not only engage your subconscious mind to work for you, you'll also engage the Creative Power of the universe that knows everything there is to know, including what is best for you.

Never entertain failure. Never complain of "hard times." In "hard times" you will find the greatest opportunities. You can create whatever you want. If you learn to overcome your fear, you will be successful in spite of your difficulties. People who are engaged daily in a vocation they love are happy people because they have happy thoughts. Happiness is an inside job.

Volumes have been written on the secret to happiness. We have all read numerous stories of how to find happiness. Here is one that spoke most clearly to me. In the old days, there was a king who was so miserable and unhappy that he called together all his soothsayers, magicians, and court advisors to find a remedy. They tried all sorts of methods to arouse the king out of his deep despair; but alas, to no avail.

Finally, one of them suggested that they search for the happiest man in the kingdom for it was thought if the king could put on the man's undershirt, the king would be happy, too. In time, they found the happiest man in the kingdom, but he had never owned an undershirt.

His happiness came from within, from the thoughts that occupied his mind day by day.

The story illustrates happiness is not something to be put on like an undershirt. It's to be found within. It comes from the thoughts that occupy your mind daily. You can create happiness by spending some time every morning counting your blessings. As you count your many blessings, you will discover life is phenomenal. It's a magnificent journey. By using more of your mental and emotional potential, you'll be able to go anywhere, do anything, and achieve anything.

Your future days on this planet can be your most exciting days ever. Do you realize, daily you have the opportunity to see the impossible become possible in every field of human endeavor? You can experience the limitless magnificence of what humans are capable of doing in sports, health, art, technology, science, and all other fields. And the best part is you can be happy and experience all the joy you can possibly hold. You can embrace your own prosperity and enjoy it. In fact, you will be so elated that you will want everyone else to experience the joy you feel.

CHAPTER 18

The More You Help Others to Be Prosperous, the More Prosperous You will Become

Our rewards in life will always be in direct proportion to our contributions. This is a Law of Economics that stands as a supporting structure to the science of Prosperity. Unfortunately, many people cannot take advantage of this wonderful law because they focus only on themselves. They are simply stuck on one side of the equation. All they have to do is start contributing to others and additional rewards will come naturally.

You can get everything you need in life without taking anything away from anyone else. There is an ample supply for everyone who really wants it. In fact, getting your own desires met puts you in a position to increase the general well-being of everyone you meet. You can rejoice in your own prosperity and in the prosperity of others.

It is good to rejoice in the prosperity of others. By rejoicing, you share in another's good fortune and, in turn, invite good fortune into your own life. Once you become prosperous, you must allow your own prosperity to circulate freely. Prosperity comes into your life and flows out of your life. As stated previously, prosperity is like the ocean tide. The ebb and flow of the tide is constant. When the tide is out, you can be absolutely sure it will come in. If you don't reach down and pull up those less fortunate, the day will come when due to sheer weight of numbers; those less fortunate will reach up and pull you down. We don't have to live long before we discover there are two planes of life that we can work on. One is the competition plane; the other, the creative plane. People on the competitive plane feel supply is limited; therefore, you are in competition with everyone else. On the creative plane prosperity is for everyone. There are no limits in life. Life is abundant. Cooperation is the key. Everyone can have their desires met. You are in competition with no one. If what you want for yourself you want for everyone else, your life will take on new meaning and purpose.

In *Einstein: The Life and Times* by Ronald W. Clark, Einstein questions the purpose of life: "Man is here for the sake of other men only."[29] We are here to serve others because it is in serving others that we will find real and lasting prosperity.

Years ago on the television series *The Twilight Zone*, a man awoke to discover he was the most prosperous man on earth. There was only one problem. He was the only person left on earth. He had everything but had no one to share it with. The man concluded that a life that has everything but no one to share it with is hell.

People who enjoy prosperity have discovered the Law of Circulation, the Law of Giving and Receiving. Emerson said: "Beware of holding too much good in your hands."[30]

Because of the unity underlying all of life, no person lives entirely to themselves. When your thoughts rest entirely upon yourself, you become discontented and unhappy. The psychological label for this type of illness is narcissism named after a misguided youth in Greek legend who pined away for love of his own image. If you have ever known a narcissistic person, you will agree with me it is not a pretty sight. To become prosperous, one must give up narcissism. All greed, suspicion, jealousy, and intolerance must be abandoned. You must find some altruistic purpose into which you can pour your life, and you'll find the happiness of which you have always dreamed.

Prosperity is to be enjoyed. What good would prosperity be if you could not enjoy it? Logan Pearsall Smith wrote, "There are two things in life to aim for: first, get what you want; second, enjoy it. Only the wisest of mankind achieves the second."[31] A state of joy is the greatest achievement of success.

You must learn to enjoy what you have. When you do, you'll find more and more coming into your life. Enjoy what you have. To pursue prosperity without enjoying it is like being caught on a treadmill. You are moving but getting nowhere.

Beware of focusing on what you don't have. Since life is far from perfect—at least insofar as perfect is created in your imagination—there is always going to be something missing. By enjoying what you have, you'll discover that whatever is missing will have a tendency to appear in your life.

The prosperity enjoyed by many is rarely covered in the media, which inundates us with "gloom and doom" and gives us constant news of fresh disasters. Anything new and gloomy sells and gets better ratings. Therefore, an incessant feast of horror is prepared for us daily by the media.

By the time a child is ten years old, he or she has witnessed 100,000 acts of violence and 8,000 murders on television. We have the image in our minds that people would just as soon kill each other as exist together. I haven't even mentioned the horror films or the school shootings. Do you see what we are feeding our minds? It is pretty scary, isn't it? Daily we hear people talk about crime, or what a cruel world this is, or how terrible their life is. It is not surprising that many people meet every day after work at the "Ain't It Awful Lounge" just to tell others how terrible their lives are. If they venture to give the listeners equal time, they will top the other person's tragedy. It's a mystery to me why we call this "Happy Hour." No doubt it's because happiness is what we're trying to achieve, but how many achieve it in this way? We don't understand that dissatisfaction generates negative energy which will result in more and more dissatisfaction until we make the course corrections needed in our lives. Let me tell you how you can achieve happiness. Volumes have been written on the secret of happiness, and everyone concludes by saying that true and lasting happiness comes from within. I'm sure you will agree we cannot enjoy life until we are happy. Most of us know what happiness is. We felt happy when we graduated from college, when we got married, when our children were born, or when we won some great victory. But these experiences are transitory. How can we find true and lasting happiness?

The late William James, father of American Psychology, said, "True and lasting happiness will come the day you get the clear realization that you can overcome any weakness—the day you realize your subconscious can solve your problems, heal your body, and prosper you beyond your wildest dreams."[32] If you are living in alignment with your values, inner peace and happiness will result. You will feel like you are living your purpose and you will be.

Happiness is a state of mind. You can choose to be happy by thinking on the right things instead of thinking on the latest gossip or how cruel life is. If you want to be happy and enjoy life, you will have to think on good things.

Some philosophers say that happiness is a habit. There is a wonderful story that comes out of the West Coast of Ireland. A man was a guest in a farmer's home in Ireland. The host was singing, whistling, and full of good humor. He was so joyous his visitor asked him the secret of his happiness. The farmer responded, "It is a habit with me. Every morning when I awaken and every night before I go to sleep I bless my family, the crops, the cattle, and I thank God for a wonderful harvest which I've had year after year for forty years."

Listen carefully to the Irish farmer's secret. Thoughts repeated regularly and systematically sink into the subconscious mind and become reality. Happiness is a habit. The happier you are, the more you are able to enjoy life.

CHAPTER 19

Enjoy Your Prosperity with Careful, Pleasurable Spending

You now know how to live and how to achieve prosperity. But do you know how to enjoy your prosperity? Too many people feel it is frivolous to spend any of their wealth on personal pleasures. The outside world has placed so much emphasis on selfishness that some people feel guilty when they purchase something for themselves. They go through life without vacations and entertainment. They refuse to do anything for themselves. If you think spending a little on yourself is immoral, you have some mental work to do. In fact, this kind of thinking will create for you a poverty consciousness. We all know people who are so stingy they can't enjoy life. Joe, a friend of mine who died a few years back, was extremely cautious about every penny he spent. Everyone who knew him jokingly said, "Old Joe has the first dollar he earned." Joe remained a bachelor. He said he wasn't going to get married until he could afford it. He always ate at home and refused to give birthday or Christmas presents to his family or friends. He considered giving gifts frivolous. He saved every penny he could and put it in a passbook savings account. Joe was afraid to take any risks. Inflation slowly decreased his savings and he ended up as some people do in retirement with a small savings account and a social security check.

Here is what happened to Joe. Joe developed a poverty consciousness by economizing all the time. He started out with nothing, and when he retired he still had most of it.

If Joe would have learned to take some risks, he could have had all the good things in life. If he could have realized that his Creator had provided infinite wealth and a part of it was for Joe's personal use, he would have spent some of his money on himself and some on others. He could have enjoyed so much more of life.

In fact, Joe could have lived in a world peopled with friends who loved him, and he could have been surrounded by beautiful things had he believed in abundance. Instead Joe allowed his fears to control him. Don't allow your fears to control you. You have the ability to transcend all previous fears and rise above them, but you can't triumph over previous fears if you insist on hanging on to old mental fears of poverty. To improve your circumstances, you must get rid of old fears and let your mind heal. You can replace fear with faith. Claim every day that the Creator of all abundance is ready to more than supply your every need. Enjoy life. Enjoy what you have. Share with others and don't forget to treat yourself with some pleasurable spending. It's okay to like money, just don't fall in love with it.

CHAPTER 20

Prosperous People Like Money, They Just Don't Fall in Love with It

Money is a symbol of exchange. It is the medium through which people exchange their production of goods and services to others. It has taken many forms throughout history—gold, bricks, silver bars, beads, and trinkets. Today we use what we call "plastic." It is more convenient to pay for something with a credit card than it is to carry around gold, silver, or livestock to exchange for whatever we wish to purchase.

Money is the measure of value that people place on goods and services. The amount of money you earn in a competitive market is the measure of value that others place on your contribution. Since money is a huge part of our everyday lives, let's put money into perspective. It is not the root of all evil. The *love* of money is the root of all evil. It is okay to like money as long as you don't fall in love with it.

When you set your heart exclusively on money, give all your attention to amassing money, and nothing else matters, you have fallen in love with money. Money is to be valued among all the other important things in life. However, there are so many more important things than money—things like your desire to express and use your talent, your desire to find your true place in life, your love of family and friends, and the joy that comes from contributing to the happiness of others.

A prosperous life is a balanced life. You can have billions of dollars, but your billions will do you no good if you don't have peace of mind, harmony, health, and the fulfillment that comes from the expression and use of the talents given you.

Prosperous people like money. They use it wisely, constructively, and judiciously. Money is constantly circulating in their lives. They release it with joy, knowing it will come back to them multiplied in wonderful ways. They use money for good, and they are grateful for the opportunity to do good. They believe whatever they do, they will prosper.

They use their subconscious mind and the creative power of their thoughts to attract a constant supply of money into their lives. They know that the real riches of life are in their minds. They know money is neither good nor bad, but thinking about it in either light makes it so. They have learned they can't get something for nothing. They must give to receive. They give attention to their goals, ideals, enterprises, and to the needs of others. It isn't surprising that they are prosperous.

People who say they have no interest in prosperity usually end up in poverty. People who say they have no interest in prosperity usually condemn prosperity silently or verbally. They have adopted the belief that there is some virtue in poverty. This subconscious belief may have come about because of early childhood training or it may be based on a false interpretation of scripture. Thus, they end up in poverty.

The great religions of the world help people erase all thoughts of evil and sin from their minds. They teach nothing happens on the outside unless something corresponding to it happens on the inside. Everything comes to us through the Law of Attraction. You cannot attract riches if you hold thoughts of poverty. This is why those who say they have no interest in prosperity will end up in poverty. They do not realize a Divine Parent would surely desire prosperity for all their children. What you think in your mind and feel deep in your heart will be what you experience in life. Why is it that out of all the people who seek prosperity only a few find it? Could it be that although many people feel they deserve a bigger income and a good life, they silently or openly condemn prosperity? You will often hear them refer to money as "filthy lucre." They say to their children that "money is the root of all evil." They don't realize whatever you condemn takes wings and flees from you. Inwardly as people condemn money, their subconscious mind will work to make sure they do not have money.

Let's review: As previously stated, the power of your subconscious can work for you or against you. Once you understand the power of your subconscious, you can engage a power that will work to make you prosperous physically, spiritually, mentally, and financially. Once you learn how to use this power, you will never be in want. All your needs will be met. You will discover the ability to perform miracles sleeps within you.

CHAPTER 21

How Prosperity Thinking Works

In summary, here's how Prosperity Thinking works. What you think in your mind and feel deep in your heart will be what you experience in life. Your subconscious mind will work for you or against you. First, let's examine how your mind can work against you. You've heard people say, "Anyone who makes a lot of money has to be some kind of crook—swindler, thief, drug dealer, or someone who cons innocent people out of their last dime. No one wants to be like that."

They are right in concluding no one wants to be like that, but look at what their subconscious mind has accepted. Their subconscious mind has accepted the idea that anyone who makes a lot of money is a crook. Their subconscious mind works to chase away the prosperity they desire. Just look at the paradox going on in this person's mind. "I wish wealth to flow to me." But the next thought is "Wealth is a dirty, evil thing." The person's subconscious mind, not wanting anything to do with evil things, heads down the road to poverty and lack. You can reverse all this by pushing these erroneous thoughts out of your conscious mind and start believing that prosperity will flow into your life. See yourself being prosperous, happy, and sharing your prosperity with others.

What have we learned about prosperity? Thinking prosperity thoughts will attract prosperity to you far more quickly than working a twelve-hour day and diligently saving every penny. The journey to prosperity is paved with strong positive affirmations held constantly in your mind, eventually attracting abundance into your life. Your thinking and inner feelings about prosperity will determine whether or not you will have prosperity. Prosperity Thinking people know there is plenty of everything to go around. They work hard to achieve prosperity so they will have plenty to share with others. They do not fall into the common trap of believing that there isn't enough for everyone. There are billions of dollars in the United States Treasury and you deserve your fair share. The supply is not limited. Prosperity-thinking people are good examples to others. They circulate what they have, knowing there is plenty for everyone. They don't worry about an economic crisis. They know people have become prosperous in every economic situation.

Prosperity-thinking people know as they use the power of their subconscious mind in a creative way, they will discover ideas that form the foundation of all fortunes. Once you decide what you desire in life, you will put into motion a force that will go out into the universe in all directions to help you accomplish your goal. Keep a prosperity attitude as your subconscious mind helps you accomplish goal after goal. Opportunities are open everywhere to those who take the time to feed their subconscious with positive affirmations of prosperity.

It's okay to feel good about yourself as you experience joy on your journey to prosperity. Often people firmly established at the height of prosperity will look back on the times of struggle as some of the happiest years of their life. In other words, achieving prosperity is fun. Enjoyment for the most part is to be found in the journey. As you travel, you will, no doubt, find others traveling a parallel journey. As long as your paths run parallel, enjoy them. Realize that after you round the next curve, there will be other people making the same journey. Stay focused and enjoy the journey. Take your fate out of the hands of chance by consciously realizing the conditions which you desire to see manifested in your life can be accomplished through Prosperity Thinking.

Meet the world with a smile. You owe this to yourself and others. Always remember you will attract what you give out. Keep smiling. It may take a little effort at first, but keep it up and it will become spontaneous. Years ago in Hollywood, the producers would tell actors to register joy and hold it! Put a smile on your face and hold it. Joy will come into your life as you develop a higher consciousness. It comes from developing a harmonious relationship with your inner self. You have taken the first step. You have decided you want a prosperous life. All things you want in life, including joy, will follow your thoughts automatically. Don't forget the spiritual aspect of your life. It must be sustained and cared for if you want to become truly prosperous. Carl Jung, one of the most brilliant psychiatrists of all time, stressed the need to develop a higher psychic function to achieve wholeness and joy. The spiritual aspects of our personality are as vital to our lives as food and water. Albert Einstein said to not give credence to the spiritual life is to deny the validity of human experience.

Whatever Spirit you have will express itself through you. This Spirit we are referring to is in every living being, in every soul. It is simply waiting to be brought forth. The Spirit can bring out the great realities of life including happiness, health, love, power, and joy. The Spirit empowers the things that make life worthwhile.

You can point the world to prosperity if you are overflowing with joy! The world sees too many joyless faces; some with that resigned look that seems to say "One rebuff more or less makes no difference. I am so sad nothing matters. I just have to bear it."

Your joy can help others realize they have a power within that can change everything. You will show them they can conquer the depression that robs them of all joy, and use the power of the Law of Attraction to attract good things into their lives. You will enhance their lives exponentially. But that's not the end of the story. You will benefit. People who are joyous will find themselves surrounded by people who are joyful and life will be prosperous. Again, the Law of Attraction is at work. Happy people attract happy people.

People are looking for joy, for a more abundant expression of life. Joy-filled persons find fault with no one and moreover find no fault with themselves. Joyous people never condemn others because they want others to enjoy life as much as they do. Now that you are prosperous, go out and spread joy to others. Your very presence will cheer people and lift them up as new life flows through your community, your society, and your world. You'll be so glad you have journeyed to prosperity.

Are you ready to put some more cash in your pocket? Are you ready to help your subconscious mind bring to you the wealth and prosperity you desire? Are you ready to enjoy the best health you have ever known? Are you ready to experience relationships at the highest level? Are you ready to finally know peace of mind? I know you are! Go out and become as prosperous as you can. Share with others and enjoy the life you have been given. You'll be so glad you did!

ENDNOTES

Chapter 1

1. Brooks Atkinson, Ed. 2000, "History," *The Essential Writings of Ralph Waldo Emerson*, New York: The Modern Library, 115.
2. Alfred Lord Tennyson, "For I Dipt Into the Future (Locksley Hall)", in *Poems That Live Forever,* selected by Hazel Felleman New York: Doubleday, 1965, 432
3. John Milton, *Paradise Lost: Book I,* New York: Barnes and Noble Classics, 2004, 19
4. Stanley Wells and Gary Taylor, eds. 1991, *William Shakespeare, Henry V, Act IV, Scene 3,* Oxford: Clarendon Press, 588

Chapter 2

1. Napoleon Hill, 1937. *Think and Grow Rich,* New York: Fawcett Books, 20
2. Frank Lloyd Wright's response to a *New York Times Magazine* reporter on October 4, 1953

Chapter 3

1. William James, 1907. *Pragmatism: A New name for Some Old Ways of Thinking,* New York: Barnes and Noble, *ix*

Chapter 4

1. Brooks Atkinson, ed. 2000. "Self-Reliance", *The Essential Writings of Ralph Waldo Emerson,* 132
2. Joseph Murphy, 2000. The Power of Your Subconscious Mind, New York: Reward Books, 37

3. Blaise Pascal quoted in Wayne Dyer, 1998. *Wisdom of the Ages.* New York: HarperCollins Publishers, 1

Chapter 5

1. Walter Isaacson, 2007. *Einstein: His Life and Universe.* New York: Simon and Schuster, 7

Chapter 6

1. Walter Isaacson, *Einstein: His Life and Universe,* 387
2. Richard Whelan, ed. 1991. *Self-Reliance: The Wisdom of Ralph Waldo Emerson as Inspiration for Daily Living,* New York: Three Rivers Press, 71
3. Wayne W. Dyer, 1995, *Your Sacred Self,* New York: Harper Paperback, 155

Chapter 7

1. Ernest Holmes, 1938, *The Science of Mind,* New York: Jeremy Tarcher/Putnam, 586

Chapter 10

1. Emmet Fox, 1968, *Power Through Constructive Thinking,* New York: HarperSanFrancisco, 126
2. Earl Nightingale, 1993, *The Essence of Success,* Niles, Illinois: Nightingale-Conant Corporation, 9
3. Brooks Atkinson,ed., *The Essential Writings of Ralph Waldo Emerson, 132*
4. George Bernard Shaw quoted in Marta Hiatt, 2007, *Mind Magic,* Woodbury, Minnesota: Llewellyn Publications, 67
5. Gautama Buddha quoted in Friedrich Max Muller, ed. 2009, *The Teachings of the Buddha,* New York: Fall River Press, 2

Chapter 11

1. Carl Sandberg, "Kansas Sodbuster", told in Earl Nightingale, 1993, *The Essence of Success,* 220-1
2. John Milton, *Paradise Lost,* 19
3. Seneca quote taken from Frank S. Mead, ed. 2000, *12,000 Inspirational*

Quotations: A Treasury of Spiritual Insights and Practical Wisdom, Springfield, Massachusetts: Federal Street Press, 305

4. Earl Nightingale, *The Essence of Success,* 282

Chapter 15

1. Milton Mayeroff, 1971, *On Caring,* New York: HarperPerennial, 104
2. Oscar Wilde, 1916, *The Prose of Oscar Wilde,* New York: Cosmopolitan Book Corporation, 601

Chapter 17

1. Earl Nightingale, 1993, *The Essence of Success,* 337
2. Earl Nightingale, *The Essence of Success,* 340

Chapter 18

1. Ronald W. Clark, 2007, *Einstein: The Life and Times,* New York: HarperCollins, Publishers, 194
2. Brooks Atkinson, *The Essential Writings of Ralph Waldo Emerson,* 164
3. Logan Pearsall Smith quoted in John-Roger and Peter McWilliams, 1992, *Wealth 101: Getting What You Want—Enjoying What You've Got,* Los Angeles, California: Prelude Press, 70
4. Joseph Murphy, *The Power of Your Subconscious Mind,* 171

www.ingramcontent.com/pod-product-compliance
Lightning Source LLC
Chambersburg PA
CBHW020012050426
42450CB00005B/435